CRYPTOCURRENCY MILLIONAIRE

Make Money With Cryptocurrency

By
Sir Patrick Bijou

CRYPTOCURRENCY MILLIONAIRE

The trademarks that are used are without any consent, and the publication of the trademark is without permission or backing by the trademark owner. All trademarks and brands within this book are for clarifying purposes only and are the owned by the owners themselves, not affiliated with this document.

ISBN 978-1-9993023-0-6

TABLE OF CONTENT

CHAPTER ONE

Introduction

Navigating the world of crypto can be very daunting due to vast usage of computing jargon and technical concepts that will almost certainly confuse you. Add to that the relative infancy of the technology, it can be hard finding structured resources to assist you in your journey.

There's a lot of excitement about Bitcoin and cryptocurrencies. We hear about startups, investments, meetups, and even buying pizza with Bitcoin. Optimists claim that Bitcoin will fundamentally alter payments, economics, and even politics around the world. Pessimists claim Bitcoin is inherently broken and will suffer an inevitable and spectacular collapse.

Importance of Performing Your Own Analysis.

For traditional investments such as stocks, fundamental analysis entails evaluating the financial health and viability of a company according to its financial statements. If the numbers look good, we can be confident that the company has good fundamentals and we can therefore invest in it. Performing fundamental analysis for cryptocurrencies however, is radically different since there are no financial statements. Why?

Because:

1) Cryptocurrencies are not corporations, but rather representations of value or assets within a network. Its viability is not based on generating a revenue, but rather directly depends on the participation of the community (users, miners and developers). Each cryptocurrency is a manifestation of the different applications of Blockchain technology, and are usually decentralized;

2) The crypto space is in its infancy stages, and almost all of the cryptocurrencies are in development stages. Which means that there are limited uses cases in the real world currently and therefore, a lack of track record to show for.

Thus, fundamental analysis on crypto must be performed with a different methodology. Given the complex nature of crypto and their underlying technology, it is even more important for us to engage in research to assess the viability and potential of the coins.

This ensures that we make better investment decisions and are kept in the loop of things. But more importantly, a good understanding of a coin's fundamentals allows you to form your own opinions and have your own stand, which is rare in the crypto world due to its complexity.

It is scary how many people begin investing in crypto without a solid understanding of investing basics or the underlying technology that works as the basis for cryptocurrency and the blockchain.

What is an ICO? All your questions answered along with our insider tips that we use to continuously pick winning projects. More on cryptocurrency and ICO investing. At the end of the day we are investors and we are here to teach you how to make money while everyone else loses it.

What is Money Anyway?

Since societies transitioned from a barter economy to using a money as a medium of exchange, individuals have tried to devise systems that allow for rational ways to exchange value. In order to help make goods and services commensurable the Greek philosopher Aristotle came up with four criteria that help to dictate what is considered to be 'good money' (Lee, 2009):

1. It must be durable
2. It must be portable
3. It must be divisible
4. It must have intrinsic value

Originally the preferred medium of exchange was gold as it was able to fulfill all four of these criteria. As economies grew and the demand for a medium of exchange increased, governments were forced to create a more accessible medium of exchange that they could control and regulate. This was the birth of fiat currency. This particular medium of exchange has been adopted worldwide, however it has come with its own set of issues.

In order to help fix some of these issues, cryptocurrencies began to emerge in 2009, leveraging a disruptive technology called blockchain.

A cryptocurrency is a digital currency that uses cryptography for security (Investopedia, 2016). Blockchain specifically deals with the way in which data is structured and allows for the existence of decentralized digital ledgers where single organizations are not able to effect transactions (Hackett, 2016). Currently the two most widely adopted cryptocurrencies are Bitcoin and Ether, the currency that is used to power the Ethereum blockchain.

The Investment

With the recent rise in popularity of cryptocurrencies many investors are now trying to determine how to invest into this new asset class. As with any investment into a new technology there are many factors to consider when assessing their future. In order to make an informed decision one must look at the origins of the technology as well as the potential applications and limitations in the foreseeable future.

Evaluating what's the price (in USD) of Bitcoin (BTC) and Ether (ETH) will be in the next 5 years using thorough quantitative and qualitative analysis. From this evaluation a decision will be made on an appropriate investment allocation between the two currencies for this crypto-portfolio.

The Contenders

Bitcoin is the most widely known and used cryptocurrency in the world. The current market capitalization of just over $10 billion (USD) (Crypto-Currency Market Capitalizations, 2016). Bitcoin was originally developed by Satoshi Nakamoto as a strictly peer-to-peer electronic payment system and a solution to the problem of double-spending (Nakamoto, 2008). It is primarily designed to eliminate the need of financial institutions or 'trusted third-party' entities. Bitcoin does this by eliminating the possibility of fraud, increasing efficiencies, and providing objective proof-of-work to guarantee validity and security in any transaction (Nakamoto, 2008). The use of a public ledger as well as digital signatures allow for a secure and anonymous transaction without the need for trust, as the public network of nodes validates transactions through finding a consensus among a majority of nodes. Thus far, the primary use cases for Bitcoin revolve around increasing efficiencies and eliminating unnecessary time and costs that arrive from using multiple trusted third parties to facilitate transactions (Tapscott, 2016). Bitcoin is highly adoptable in markets that are lacking in traditional financial infrastructure but have access to mobile data, as well as markets with highly inflated currencies that require tools to allow for the mobilization and exchange of currencies (Magee, 2015). Bitcoin's multiversion concurrency control is unique and allows for safe concurrent transactions without significant delay (Greenspan, 2015).

Ethereum's main point of differentiation is the ability to leverage the application of 'smart contracts' within its code. While growing at a much more significant rate over the past year, Ethereum has a total market capitalization of only approximately 10% of Bitcoin (Crypto-Currency Market Capitalizations, 2016). While the underlying currency, Ether, appreciates and depreciates in value, Ethereum's value is largely driven by its increased utility and ability to eventually eliminate third parties' involvement in determining contractual obligations. The main benefit of Ethereum can be found in the belief that, as long as it can be coded properly, Ethereum's smart contracts carry potentially unlimited utility (although, highly complex contracts could prove to be illogical at this point in time) (Greenspan, 2016). The Ethereum Network serves to facilitate the exchange of data, information, votes, etc. indicating that there is the possibility for use cases well beyond simply serving as a disruptor to the current financial institutions. The Ether currency serves as the 'gas' that powers the transactions within the Ethereum Network. Ethereum leverages a Turing-Complete language which could, in theory, solve any computational problem (DeRose, 2016), allowing for an even greater possibility for utility across many areas

Both Ether and Bitcoin are mined by solving highly complex computational problems. Additionally, as more blocks are mined, the difficulty of finding new blocks increases in both cases.

Sir Patrick Bijou

Comparison: Where Bitcoin currently has a clearly defined use case in which disruption is possible, the possibilities for Ethereum to enter the market are far less distinct. Ethereum benefits from the possibility of much greater eventual impact. Bitcoin is currently better positioned to leverage and be incorporated into innovations that occur across many industries, whereas Ethereum is trying to drive the innovations. Ethereum is at a greater risk of experiencing disruption, as their network is the major driver of value (while the Ether 'gas' simply drives the network). This network which drives innovation opens up Ethereum to be disrupted by future entrants looking to build upon the existing framework. Bitcoin is largely safe from this threat of new entrants as Bitcoin's explicit purpose of acting as a digital currency has been effectively accomplished, where future innovative networks can use Bitcoin as an underlying asset.

Comparison of BTC and ETH

Bitcoin: Ethereum:

Explicit niche, limited range of uses,	Use of 'smart contracts', versatile,
MVCC, more widely adopted,	Ethereum Virtual Machine, Turing-
leverages	complete, dramatic growth, IoT,
innovation	innovation driver, blockchain 2.0

Shared Traits:

Cryptocurrencies, anonymous, no need for 'trust', blocks are 'mined' with increasing difficulty, underlying use of blockchain technology.

Will History Repeat Itself?

Using historical data to forecast values of both Bitcoin and Ethereum in five years proved to be very difficult, as there was insufficient data to project future prices with confidence. When examining the trends in both sets of prices, the 5 year forecast for Bitcoin is $2550 which represents growth of 301%, while Ethereum's forecasted value is approximately $88, which represents growth of 634%. Both values represent absolutely incredible growth rates due in large part to the dramatic growth driven by hype and adoption in the early stage of the life cycle.

Upon further analysis, the high growth and volatility of both Bitcoin and Ethereum are the result of news, hype, and speculation. This is shown by the extremely high correlation between prices and Google searches for each respective currency. When looking at Bitcoin the time-series correlation between price and Google searches for "Bitcoin" is 0.64, while Ethereum's correlation is even higher than that, at 0.88. In order to account for the hype in our regression forecast, the significance of spikes resulting from increased hype and Google searches were discounted by a factor of 30%. As can be seen in the following figure, prices are significantly depressed when the hype and speculation surrounding each currency is decreased by 30%. The depressed impact of Google searches led to a growth rate for Bitcoin of approximately 300% while Ethereum's is reduced to 506%. Although the reduced importance of hype and speculation does lessen this forecast, Ethereum has clearly experienced more growth in the recent past.

Cryptocurrency Millionaire

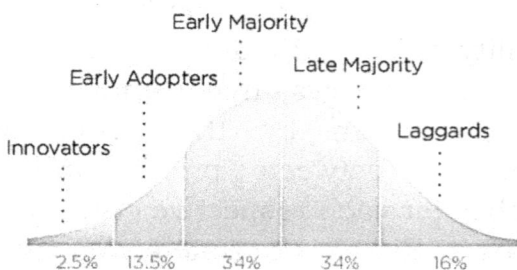

INNOVATION ADOPTION LIFECYCLE

Image: Wikipedia

CHAPTER TWO

Is Blockchain technology the new internet?

The blockchain is an absolutely ingenious invention - the brainchild of a person or group whose names are undisclosed and go by the pseudonym, Satoshi Nakamoto. Since then it has been evolving into something much larger and yet everyone is still asking the question:

Mechanics of Bitcoin

Blockchain technology creates the backbone of a new type of internet by allowing digital information to be distributed but not copied. It was originally created for the digital currecy, Bitcoin however it is much more than that today and is being used by technology companies across the globe in a plethora of projects.

Bitcoin the "digital gold" has a total currency value of near 42 billion US. Blockchains aren't limited to this framework however and can make other types of digital value. Like the internet you don't exactly need to know how it works to use it. However, it is always better to have at least a basic knowledge of any technology you wish to be involved in to understand why it's considered revolutionary.

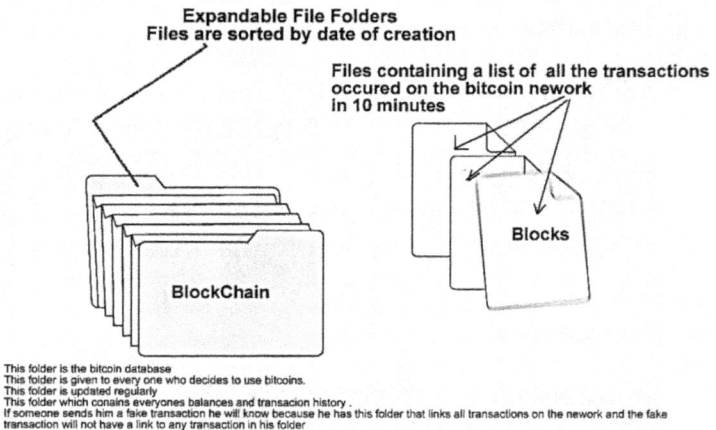

Expandable File Folders
Files are sorted by date of creation

Files containing a list of all the transactions occured on the bitcoin nework in 10 minutes

Blocks

BlockChain

This folder is the bitcoin database
This folder is given to every one who decides to use bitcoins.
This folder is updated regularly
This folder which conains everyones balances and transacion history .
If someone sends him a fake transaction he will know because he has this folder that links all transactions on the nework and the fake transaction will not have a link to any transaction in his folder

A new database

Imagine this: A spreadsheet that is duplicated thousands of times across a network of computers. Then imagine that this network is designed to regularly update this spreadsheet so each version of the spreadsheet is always identical. In essence that is the blockchain.

The information on a blockchain exists as a continually shared and reconciled database.

There are some obvious benefits that come from this structure. The database isn't stored in any single location, meaning the records are always kept truly public which makes verification easy. There are no centralized versions of this information that hackers could potentially ultra or corrupt. Hosted by millions of computers all the time, the data is accessible to anyone on the internet.

Blockchain robustness and durability

Blockchain technology is often compared to the internet in its early days in that it has a built-in robustness. By storing its information across the entire network the blockchain cannot:

1. Be controlled or manipulated by any single entity.
2. Has no single point of failure.

Bitcoin was created in 2008 and since that time the Bitcoin blockchain has operated without any significant disruptions which is a very formidable proof of concept. (To date, any problems associated with Bitcoin have been due to hacking or mismanagement. In other words, these problems come from bad intention and human error, not flaws in the underlying concepts.) It's predecessor 'the internet' has itself proven to be durable now for almost 30 years which is a track record that signals good things for blockchain tech as it continues to evolve.

"As revolutionary as it sounds, Blockchain truly is a mechanism to bring everyone to the highest degree of accountability. No more missed transactions, human or machine errors, or even an exchange that was not done with the consent of the parties involved. Above anything else, the most critical area where Blockchain helps is to guarantee the validity of a transaction by recording it not only on a main register but a connected distributed system of registers, all of which are connected through a secure validation mechanism."

Business Opportunities Hidden Inside the Bitcoin Landscape

The Bitcoin industry as a whole. It's important to familiarize yourself with the industry analysis since one of the main questions you should ask yourself when deciding on your Bitcoin business is, "Where is the industry headed?"

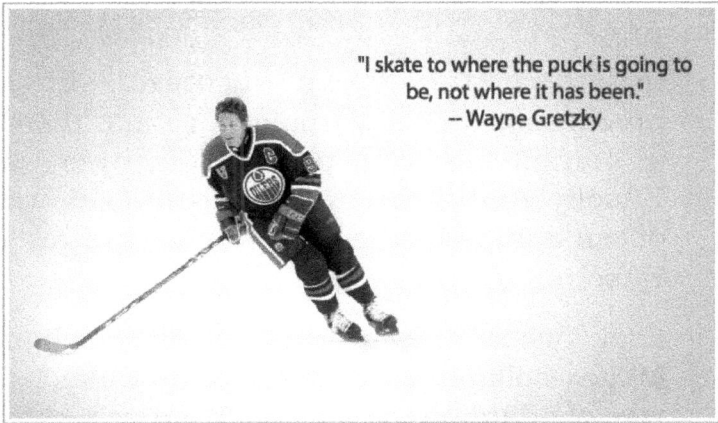

"I skate to where the puck is going to be, not where it has been."
-- Wayne Gretzky

You shouldn't try to figure out what's hot right now, but rather predict what will be the next hot thing and target it before everyone else.

Creating your Bitcoin business, There are specific tools and techniques to figure this out. But for now let's focus on what data we can find on the Bitcoin industry today.

As we near the middle of there are currently:

Over 8.5 million Bitcoin wallets

Over 88,000 merchants that accept Bitcoin

374 Bitcoin ATM machines

More than $676 million invested in Bitcoin startups through venture capital

103 VC (venture capital) backed start-ups

In order to create a successful Bitcoin business you need to make sure that there is a market for you product, in this case Bitcoin. And if the price goes up or down it doesn't matter, there is still a market for Bitcoin.

Even when the biggest Bitcoin exchange MTgox collapsed in 2014 it didn't affect the rate of adoption for Bitcoin. There is a steady increase in the number Bitcoin wallets opened each year and even though the price may be lower than last year the adoption rate is still positive. The price decline has not stopped the exchange trading volume from trending up.

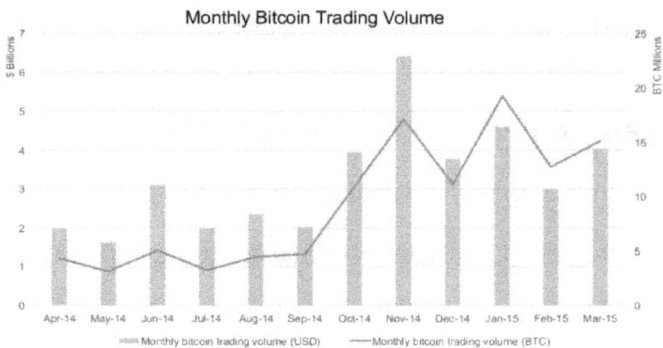

Monthly Bitcoin Trading Volume

Data sources: Blockchain, CoinDesk, Bitparity

Finally, since the Bitcoin price has dropped but mining difficulty remained more or less the same, the incentive to mine Bitcoins has diminished and less people are dealing with home mining and mining is becoming more consolidated.

Using the Bitcoin protocol to disrupt industries worldwide.

Bitcoin has certain rules, also known as the Bitcoin protocol, which makes it work. The ingenious part of Bitcoin is not necessarily the creation of the currency but rather the creation of the Bitcoin protocol. For the first time in history, technology makes it possible to transfer property rights (such as shares, certificates, digital money, etc.) in a fast, transparent and very secure way.

Moreover, these transactions can take place without the involvement of a trusted intermediary such as a government, notary, or bank. Companies and governments are no longer needed as the "middle man" in all kinds of financial agreements.

Using the Bitcoin protocol to create Bitcoin the currency is just one out of many uses you can have for this protocol. A lot of businesses are also forming around the idea of Bitcoin

2.0 - which means the decentralization of previously centralized businesses.

Some examples for Bitcoin 2.0 projects are Etherum (a platform for decentralized apps) and Gems (a sort of decentralized social messenger). Creating a Bitcoin 2.0 project also requires technical knowhow since you'll need to implement the Bitcoin protocol into other forms of assets.

Bitcoin protocol to create new products:

Email

Applications that eliminate spam by requesting a small amount of Bitcoin for every delivery. So for example let's say a "normal" person sends out 100 emails a day. If we request 10 Satoshis (the smallest amount of a Bitcoin available = 0.00000001BTC) for every email he sends he will need to pay 100 Satoshis daily or 360,500 Satoshis yearly. This is equivalent to $0.0867167 at today's exchange rate. Not too bad - paying $1 a year for email to avoid spam.

Why would this eliminate spam you ask? Well imagine that a spammer needing to pay for 100,000 emails a day - this will cost him

$1000 each year. Suddenly email spam takes a toll and isn't free to abuse as it is today.

Video

Applications that eliminate video advertising by charging a small BTC amount for the time viewed.

Crowdfunding

Global crowdfunding applications that allow project creators to raise funds easily from around the world using Bitcoin.

Payouts

Applications that allow creators or service providers to get paid by a global audience. ChangeTip is a great example of how people can tip Bitcoin to Internet users who helped them out.

Remittances

One of the hottest industries Bitcoin is trying to disrupt. Through Bitcoin you can create applications that enable worldwide, cross-border payments. Many Bitcoin startups are basically trying to "bank the unbanked".

Ecommerce

Bitcoin focused merchant directories that offer a beautiful UI for consumers.

Identity

Applications that give people control of their own identity (without the need of a 3rd party like the government).

Attribution

Applications that allow users to prove ownership of assets.

Voting

Blockchain-based technology is already being used in elections throughout the web. This way you know your vote was counted while still keeping your anonymity.

The advantages of creating a Bitcoin 2.0 business are that you are inside a blue ocean - meaning there's little competition (no sharks, unlike a red ocean) and also this is definitely the place the industry is headed.

Probably not all of what is written here makes sense to you and that's OK. Heck, it doesn't even all make sense to me sometimes. You don't need to be an expert on Bitcoin; you just need to understand the basics of where the industry is headed so you can choose your Bitcoin business idea more wisely.

One of the best sources that consolidates all the Bitcoin industry's information is Coin desk's state of Bitcoin report. This report comes out once a quarter (every three months) and sums up everything nicely. A lot of the data brought here is from that report. So make sure to sign up for report updates and keep your finger on the pulse of the Bitcoin industry.

What business opportunities lie within the Bitcoin 1.0 industry?

Since Bitcoin came to public awareness in late 2013 (when the price spiked to around $1200 for one Bitcoin) a lot of new Bitcoin businesses started to show up.

This Bitcoin boom brought in new opportunities; now not only can you open a new Bitcoin business that caters the demand of the general public who all of a sudden is interested in Bitcoin, but also you can cater for those exact same Bitcoin businesses that came about in 2014.

Simply put, two new markets have emerged: The consumer Bitcoin market and the Bitcoin businesses market. So when we say the consumer Bitcoin market, It mean the market in which you will open a Bitcoin exchange business, or a Bitcoin wallet business and your customers will be mainly consumers. This is also known as B2C - Business to Consumer.

The Bitcoin business market, it about supplying leads to Bitcoin businesses and getting paid for bringing them new customers. This is known as B2B - Business to Business

Most people tend to focus on the first market; the difference is that while the Bitcoin B2C market is larger it has way too much competition, and if you don't have a good market penetration strategy it's going to be hard to gain customers.

The Bitcoin B2B market on the other hand has almost no competition, mainly due to the fact that it's smaller. But it's still large enough to be able to profit from.

The node network

Computer connected to the blockchain network using a client that performs the task of validating and relaying transactions) gets a copy of the blockchain, which gets downloaded automatically upon joining the blockchain network.

Together these nodes create a powerful second-level network, a completely different vision for how the internet could function. To join the network each "node" is incentivised and the incentive to join the Bitcoin network is simple, the chance to win Bitcoins.

You may have heard the term "mining" Bitcoins. That term is somewhat of a misnomer. In reality what is happening is that each one is competing to earn Bitcoins by solving complex computational puzzles. Bitcoin was the raison d'etre of the blockchain as it was originally conceived. However it is now recognized as only the first of many potential applications. There is an ever growing number of Bitcoin-esque cryptocurrencies that are already available as well as a range of potential adaptations of the original blockchain concepts in development.

Decentralization, the catch phrase of crypto

There is a global network of computers (remember nodes) that use blockchain technology to manage the database that records Bitcoin transactions. Which means that bitcoin is not managed by any central authority, it is managed by the network. Decentralizition means that the network operates on a user-to-user / peer-to-peer basis, completely revolutionary.

Who will actually use the blockchain?

That is the million (trillion?) dollar question. So far finance offers the strongest use cases for the technology however we are seeing projects that do everything from gambling to buying concert tickets.

The main value proposition from blockchain is that it potentially cuts out the middle man for these types of transactions.

There is one incredibly important thing that always needs to happen before mass adoption is possible and that is a user friendly interface (GUI). This has happened rather recently with places like CoinBase and CoinJar opening up as a "wallet". The term wallet accurately describes exactly what these websites do. They store your digital money. The creation of these wallet applications now allows people to buy things with Bitcoin and store it alongside other cryptocurrencies in a user friendly and easy to do environement.

"Online identity and reputation will be decentralized. We will own the data that belongs to us."

William Mougayar, author The Business Blockchain: Promise, Practice, and Application of the Next Internet Technology (2016) Enhanced Security; The Blockchain

There is no central head of the blockchain network which eliminates the risks that inevitably come with data that is held centrally. Computer hackers can't exploit the centralized points of vulnerability. The internet that we know and love of today has security problems of its own. We all rely on the "username/password" system to protect our online identity and assets in the online world. Blockchain security methods are different.

The encryption technology basis are the so-called public and private "keys".

A public key: a long randomly-generated string of numbers is a user's personal address. Bitcoins or any other cryptocurrencies sent across the network are recorded as belonging to that address and in-turn the person that owns that address.

A private key: is more like a password that gives its owner access to the "wallet" and access to their Bitcoin or other digital assets. This makes the private key essential the username AND password for your digital assets. So it is of the utmost importance to make sure it's secure.

Many of the startups in the space will either begin generating revenue – via providing products the market demands/values – or vaporize due to running out of cash. In other words, the should be the year where there is more implementation of products utilizing blockchain technology, and less talk about blockchain tech being the magical pixie dust that can just be sprinkled atop everything. Of course, from a customer's viewpoint, this will not be obvious as blockchain technolgy should dominantly be invisible – even as its features and functionality improve peoples'/business' lives. This implementation stage, which it should represent, is a crucial step in the larger adoption of blockchain technolgy, as it will allow skeptics to see the functionality, rather than just hear of its promise."

The Blockchain a New Web 3.0?

The blockchain gives internet users the ability to create value and authenticates digital information. What new business applications will result?

Smart contracts

Distributed ledgers enable the coding of simple contracts that will execute when specified conditions are met. Ethereumis an open source blockchain project that was built specifically to realize this possibility. Still, in its early stages, Ethereum has the potential to leverage the usefulness of blockchains on a truly world-changing scale.

At the technology's current level of development, smart contracts can be programmed to perform simple functions. For instance, a derivative could be paid out when a financial instrument meets certain benchmark, with the use of blockchain technology and Bitcoin enabling the payout to be automated.

The sharing economy

With companies like Uber and AirBnB flourishing, the sharing economy is already a proven success. Currently, however, users who want to hail a ride-sharing service have to rely on an intermediary like Uber. By enabling peer-to-peer payments, the blockchain opens the door to direct interaction between parties that truly decentralized sharing economy results.

An early example, OpenBazaar uses the blockchain to create a peer-to-peer eBay. Download the app onto your computing device, and you can transact with OpenBazzar vendors without paying transaction fees. The "no rules" ethos of the protocol means that personal reputation will be even more important to business interactions than it currently is on eBay.

Crowdfunding

Crowdfunding initiatives like Kickstarter and Gofundme are doing the advance work for the emerging peer-to-peer economy. The popularity of these sites suggests people want to have a direct say in product development.

Blockchains take this interest to the next level, potentially creating crowd-sourced venture capital funds.

In 2016, one such experiment, the Ethereum-based DAO (Decentralized Autonomous Organization), raised an astonishing $200 million USD in just over two months. Participants purchased "DAO tokens" allowing them to vote on smart contract venture capital investments (voting power was proportionate to the number of DAO they were holding). A subsequent hack of project funds proved that the project was launched without proper due diligence, with disastrous consequences. Regardless, the DAO experiment suggests the blockchain has the potential to usher in "a new paradigm of economic cooperation."

Governance

By making the results fully transparent and publicly accessible, distributed database technology could bring full transparency to elections or any other kind of poll taking. Ethereum-based smart contracts help to automate the process.

The app, Boardroom, enables organizational decision-making to happen on the blockchain. In practice, this means company governance becomes fully transparent and verifiable when managing digital assets, equity or information.

Supply chain auditing

Consumers increasingly want to know that the ethical claims companies make about their products are real. Distributed ledgers provide an easy way to certify that the backstories of the things we buy are genuine. Transparency comes with blockchain-based timestamping of a date and location — on ethical diamonds, for instance — that corresponds to a product number.

The UK-based Provenance offers supply chain auditing for a range of consumer goods. Making use of the Ethereum blockchain, a Provenance pilot project ensures that fish sold in Sushi restaurants in Japan has been sustainably harvested by its suppliers in Indonesia.

File storage

Decentralizing file storage on the internet brings clear benefits. Distributing data throughout the network protects files from getting hacked or lost.

Inter Planetary File System (IPFS) makes it easy to conceptualize how a distributed web might operate. Similar to the way a bit torrent moves data around the internet, IPFS gets rid of the need for centralized client-server relationships (i.e., the current web). An internet made up of completely decentralized websites has the potential to speed up file transfer and streaming times. Such an improvement is not only convenient. It's a necessary upgrade to the web's currently overloaded content-delivery systems.

Prediction markets

The crowdsourcing of predictions on event probability is proven to have a high degree of accuracy. Averaging opinions cancels out the unexamined biases that distort judgment. Prediction markets that pay out according to event outcomes are already active. Blockchains are a "wisdom of the crowd" technology that will no doubt find other applications in the years to come.

Still, in Beta, the prediction market application Augur makes share offerings on the outcome of real-world events. Participants can earn money by buying into the correct prediction. The more shares purchased in the correct outcome, the higher the payout will be. With a small commitment of funds (less than a dollar), anyone can ask a question, create a market based on a predicted outcome, and collect half of all transaction fees the market generates.

Protection of intellectual property

As is well known, digital information can be infinitely reproduced — and distributed widely thanks to the internet. This has given web users globally a goldmine of free content. However, copyright holders have not been so lucky, losing control over their intellectual property and suffering financially as a consequence. Smart contracts can protect copyright and automate the sale of creative works online, eliminating the risk of file copying and redistribution.

Mycelia uses the blockchain to create a peer-to-peer music distribution system. Founded by the UK singer-songwriter Imogen Heap, Mycelia enables musicians to sell songs directly to audiences, as well as licence samples to producers and divvy up royalties to songwriters and musicians — all of these functions being automated by smart contracts. The capacity of blockchains to issue payments in fractional cryptocurrency amounts (micropayments) suggests this use case for the blockchain has a strong chance of success.

Internet of Things (IoT)

What is the IoT? The network-controlled management of certain types of electronic devices — for instance, the monitoring of air temperature in a storage facility. Smart contracts make the automation of remote systems management possible. A combination of software, sensors, and the network facilitates an exchange of data between objects and mechanisms. The result increases system efficiency and improves cost monitoring.

The biggest players in manufacturing, technogly and telecommunications are all vying for IoT dominance. Think Samsung, IBM and AT&T. A natural extension of existing infrastructure controlled by incumbents, IoT applications will run the gamut from predictive maintenance of mechanical parts to data analytics, and mass-scale automated systems management.

Neighbourhood Microgrids

Blockchain technology enables the buying and selling of the renewable energy generated by neighborhood microgrids. When solar panels make excess energy, Ethereum-based smart contracts automatically redistribute it. Similar types of smart contract automation will have many other applications as the IoT becomes a reality.

Located in Brooklyn, Consensys is one of the foremost companies globally that is developing a range of applications for Ethereum. One project they are partnering on is Transactive Grid, working with the distributed energy outfit, LO3. A prototype project currently up and running uses

Ethereum smart contracts to automate the monitoring and redistribution of microgrid energy. This so-called "intelligent grid" is an early example of IoT functionality.

Identity management

There is a definite need for better identity management on the web. The ability to verify your identity is the lynchpin of financial transactions that happen online. However, remedies for the security risks that come with web commerce are imperfect at best. Distributed ledgers offer enhanced methods for proving who you are, along with the possibility to digitize personal documents. Having a secure identity will also be important for online interactions — for instance, in the sharing economy. A good reputation, after all, is the most important condition for conducting transactions online.

Developing digital identity standards is proving to be a highly complex process. Technical challenges aside, a universal online identity solution requires cooperation between private entities and government. Add to that the need to navigate legal systems in different countries and the problem becomes exponentially difficult. E-Commerce on the internet currently relies on the SSL certificate (the little green lock) for secure transactions on the web. Netki is a startup that aspires to create a SSL standard for the blockchain. Having recently announced a $3.5 million seed round, Netki expects a product launch in early 2017.

AML and KYC

Anti-money laundering (AML) and know your customer (KYC) practices have a strong potential for being adapted to the blockchain. Currently, financial institutions must perform a labour intensive multi-step process for each new customer. KYC costs could be reduced through cross-institution client verification, and at the same time increase monitoring and analysis effectiveness.

Startup Polycoin has an AML/KYC solution that involves analysing transactions. Those transactions identified as being suspicious are forwarded on to compliance officers. Another startup Tradle is developing an application called Trust in Motion (TiM). Characterized as an "Instagram for KYC", TiM allows customers to take a snapshot of key documents (passport, utility bill, etc.). Once verified by the bank, this data is cryptographically stored on the blockchain.

Data management

Today, in exchange for their personal data people can use social media platforms like Facebook for free. In future, users will have the ability to manage and sell the data their online activity generates. Because it can be easily distributed in small fractional amounts, Bitcoin — or something like it — will most likely be the currency that gets used for this type of transaction.

The MIT project Enigma understands that user privacy is the key precondition for creating of a personal data marketplace. Enigma uses cryptographic techniques to allow individual data sets to be split between nodes, and at the same time run bulk computations over the data group as a whole. Fragmenting the data also makes Enigma scalable (unlike those blockchain solutions where data gets replicated on every node). A Beta launch is promised within the next six months.

Land title registration

As Publicly-accessible ledgers, blockchains can make all kinds of record-keeping more efficient. Property titles are a case in point. They tend to be susceptible to fraud, as well as costly and labour intensive to administer.

A number of countries are undertaking blockchain-based land registry projects. Honduras was the first government to announce such an initiative in 2015, although the current status of that project is unclear. This year, the Republic of Georgia cemented a deal with the Bitfury Group to develop a blockchain system for property titles. Reportedly, Hernando de Soto, the high profile economist and property rights advocate, will be advising on the project. Most recently, Sweden announced it was experimenting with a blockchain application for property titles.

Stock trading

The potential for added efficiency in share settlement makes a strong use case for blockchains in stock trading. When executed peer-to-peer, trade confirmations become almost instantaneous (as opposed to taking three days for clearance). Potentially, this means intermediaries, such as the clearing house, auditors and custodians, get removed from the process.

Numerous stock and commodities exchanges are prototyping blockchain applications for the services they offer, including the ASX (Australian Securities Exchange), the Deutsche Börse (Frankfurt's stock exchange) and the JPX (Japan Exchange Group). Most high profile because the acknowledged first mover in the area, is the Nasdaq's Linq, a platform for private market trading (typically between pre-IPO startups and investors). A partnership with the blockchain tech company Chain, Linq announced the completion of it its first share trade in 2015. More recently, Nasdaq announced the development of a trial blockchain project for proxy voting on the Estonian Stock Market.

CHAPTER THREE

What is Fiat Currency?

In the age of cryptocurrency, Wall Street journalists Paul Vigna and Michael J. Casey deliver the definitive answer to this question. Cybermoney is poised to launch a revolution, one that could entirely re- invent traditional financial and social structures while bringing the world's billions of "unbanked" individuals into a new global economy.

Cryptocurrency represents the promise of a financial system without a middleman, one owned by the people who use it and one safeguarded from the devastation of a 2008-type crash.

But bitcoin, the most famous of the cybermonies, brings with it a reputation for instability, wild fluctuation, and illicit business; some fear it has the power to eliminate jobs and to upend the concept of a nation-state. It implies, above all, monumental and wide-reaching change—for better and for worse. But it is here to stay, and you ignore it at your peril.

Vigna and Casey demystify the concept of cryptocurrency, detailing its origins, its function, and what you need to know to navigate a cyber-economy. The digital currency world will look very different from the paper currency world.

Cryptography & Cryptocurrencies

All currencies need some way to control supply and enforce various security properties to prevent cheating. In fiat currencies, organizations like central banks control the money supply and add anti-counterfeiting features to physical currency. These security features raise the bar for an attacker, but they don't make money impossible to counterfeit. Ultimately, law enforcement is necessary for stopping people from breaking the rules of the system.

Cryptocurrencies too must have security measures that prevent people from tampering with the state of the system, and from equivocating that is, making mutually inconsistent statements to different people. If

Alice convinces Bob that she paid him a digital coin, for example, she should not be able to convince Carol that she paid her that same coin. But unlike fiat currencies, the security rules of cryptocurrencies need to be enforced purely technologically and without relying on a central authority.

As the word suggests, cryptocurrencies make heavy use of cryptography. Cryptography provides a mechanism for securely encoding the rules of a cryptocurrency system in the system itself. We can use it to prevent tampering and equivocation, as well as to encode the rules for creation of new units of the currency into a mathematical protocol. Before we can properly understand cryptocurrencies then, we'll need to delve into the cryptographic foundations that they rely upon.

Cryptography is a deep academic research field utilizing many advanced mathematical techniques that are notoriously subtle and complicated to understand. Fortunately, Bitcoin only relies on a handful of relatively simple and well-known cryptographic constructions. Specifically cryptographic hashes and digital signatures, two primitives that prove to be very useful for building cryptocurrencies.

Cryptographic Hash Functions

The first cryptographic primitive that we'll need to understand is a cryptographic hash function. A hash functions as mathematical function with the following three properties:

Its input can be any string of any size.

it produces a fixed size output. For the purpose of making the discussion in this chapter concrete, we will assume a 256-bit output size. However, our discussion holds true for any output size as long as it is sufficiently large.

it is efficiently computable. Intuitively this means that for a given input string, you can figure out what the output of the hash function is in a reasonable amount of time. More technically, computing the hash of an n-bit string should have a running time that is $O(n)$.

A Simple Cryptocurrency

Now let's move from cryptography to cryptocurrencies. Eating our cryptographic vegetables will start to pay off here, and we'll gradually see how the pieces fit together and why cryptographic operations like hash functions and digital signatures are actually useful.

GoofyCoin

The first of the two is GoofyCoin, which is about the simplest cryptocurrency we can imagine. There are just two rules of GoofyCoin. The first rule is that a designated entity, Goofy, can create new coins whenever he wants and these newly created coins belong to him.

To create a coin, Goofy generates a unique coin ID unique Coin ID that he's never generated before and constructs the string "Create Coin [uniqueCoinID]". He then computes the digital signature of this string with his secret signing key. The string, together with Goofy's signature, is a coin. Anyone can verify that the coin contains Goofy's valid signature of a CreateCoin statement, and is therefore a valid coin.

The second rule of GoofyCoin is that whoever owns a coin can transfer it on to someone else. Transferring a coin is not simply a matter of sending the coin data structure to the recipient, it's done using cryptographic operations.

Assuming Goofy wants to transfer a coin that he created to Alice. To do this he creates a new statement that says "Pay this to Alice" where "this" is a hash pointer that references the coin in question. And as we saw earlier, identities are really just public keys, so "Alice" refers to Alice's public key. Finally, Goofy signs the string representing the statement. Since Goofy is the one who originally owned that coin, he has to sign any transaction that spends the coin. Once this data structure representing Goofy's transaction signed by him exists, Alice owns the coin. She can prove to anyone that she owns the coin, because she can present the data structure with Goofy's valid signature. Furthermore, it points to a valid coin that was owned by Goofy. So the validity and ownership of coins are self-evident in the system.

Once Alice owns the coin, she can spend it in turn. To do this she creates a statement that says, "Pay this coin to Bob's public key" where "this" is a hash pointer to the coin that was owned by her. And of course, Alice signs this statement. Anyone, when presented with this coin, can verify that Bob is the owner. They would follow the chain of hash pointers back to the coin's creation and verify that at each step, the rightful owner signed a statement that says "pay this coin to [new owner]".

To summarize, the rules of GoofyCoin are:

Goofy can create new coins by simply signing a statement that he's making a new coin with a unique coin ID.

Whoever owns a coin can pass it on to someone else by signing a statement that saying, "Pass on this coin to X" (where X is specified as a public key)

Anyone can verify the validity of a coin by following the chain of hash pointers back to its creation by Goofy, verifying all of the signatures along the way.

Of course, there's a fundamental security problem with GoofyCoin. Let's say Alice passed her coin on to Bob by sending her signed statement to Bob but didn't tell anyone else. She could create another signed statement that pays the very same coin to Chuck. To Chuck, it would appear that it is perfectly valid transaction, and now he's the owner of the coin. Bob and Chuck would both have valid-looking claims to be the owner of this coin. This is called a double-spending attack — Alice is spending the same coin twice. Intuitively, we know coins are not supposed to work that way.

In fact, double-spending attacks are one of the key problems that any cryptocurrency has to solve. GoofyCoin does not solve the double-spending attack and therefore it's not secure. GoofyCoin is simple, and its mechanism for transferring coins is actually very similar to Bitcoin, but because it is insecure it won't cut it as a cryptocurrency.

ScroogeCoin

To solve the double-spending problem, we'll design another cryptocurrency, which we'll call ScroogeCoin. ScroogeCoin is built off of GoofyCoin, but it's a bit more complicated in terms of data structures.

The first key idea is that a designated entity called Scrooge publishes an append-onlyledger containing the history of all the transactions that have happened. The append-only property ensures that any data written to this ledger will remain forever. If the ledger is truly append-only, we can use it to defend against double-spending by requiring all transactions to be written the ledger before they are accepted. That way, it will be publicly visible if coins were previously sent to a different owner.

To implement this append-only functionality, Scrooge can build a block chain (the data structure we discussed before) which he will digitally sign. It's a series of data blocks, each with one transaction in it (in practice, as an optimization, we'd really put multiple transactions into the same block, as Bitcoin does.) Each block has the ID of a transaction, the transaction's contents, and a hash pointer to the previous block. Scrooge digitally signs the final hash pointer, which binds all of the data in this entire structure, and publishes the signature along with the block chain.

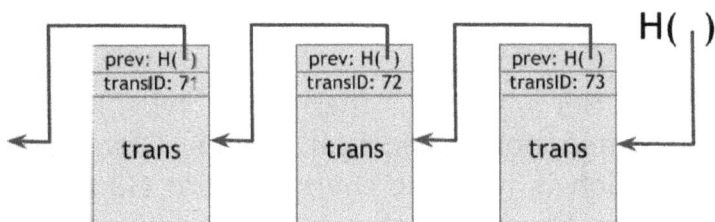

In ScroogeCoin a transaction only counts if it is in the block chain signed by Scrooge. Anybody can verify that a transaction was endorsed by Scrooge by checking Scrooge's signature on the block that it appears in. Scrooge makes sure that he doesn't endorse a transaction that attempts to double-spend an already spent coin.

Why do we need a block chain with hash pointers in addition to having Scrooge sign each block? This ensures the append-only property. If Scrooge tries to add or remove a transaction to the history, or change an existing transaction, it will affect all of the following blocks because of the hash pointers. As long as someone is monitoring the latest hash pointer published by Scrooge, the change will be obvious and easy to catch. In a system where Scrooge signed blocks individually, you'd have to keep track of every single signature Scrooge ever issued. A block chain makes it very easy for any two individuals to verify that they have observed the exact same history of transactions signed by Scrooge.

In ScroogeCoin, there are two kinds of transactions. The first kind is CreateCoins, which is just like the operation Goofy could do in GoofyCoin that makes a new coin. With ScroogeCoin, we'll extend the semantics a bit to allow multiple coins to be created in one transaction.

transID: 73	type:CreateCoins	
coins created		
num	value	recipient
0	3.2	0x...
1	1.4	0x...
2	7.1	0x...

coinID 73(0)
coinID 73(1)
coinID 73(2)

This CreateCoins transaction creates multiple coins. Each coin has a serial number within the transaction. Each coin also has a value; it's worth a certain number of ScroogeCoins. Finally, each coin has a recipient, which is a public key that gets the coin when it's created. So CreateCoins creates a bunch of new coins with different values and assigns them to people as initial owners. We refer to coins by CoinIDs. A CoinID is a combination of a transaction ID and the coin's serial number within that transaction.

A CreateCoins transaction is always valid by definition if it is signed by Scrooge. We won't worry about when Scrooge is entitled to create coins or how many, just like we didn't worry in GoofyCoin about how Goofy is chosen as the entity allowed to create coins.

The second kind of transaction is PayCoins. It consumes some coins, that is, destroys them, and creates new coins of the same total value. The new coins might belong to different people (public keys). This transaction has to be signed by everyone who's paying in a coin. So if you're the owner of one of the coins that's going to be consumed in this transaction, then you need to digitally sign the transaction to say that you're really okay with spending this coin.

transID: 73	type:PayCoins

consumed coinIDs:
68(1), 42(0), 72(3)

coins created

num	value	recipient
0	3.2	0x...
1	1.4	0x...
2	7.1	0x...

signatures

The rules of ScroogeCoin say that PayCoins transaction is valid if four things are true:

The consumed coins are valid, that is, they really were created in previous transactions.

The consumed coins were not already consumed in some previous transaction. That is, that this is not a double-spend.

The total value of the coins that come out of this transaction is equal to the total value of the coins that went in. That is, only Scrooge can create new value.

The transaction is validly signed by the owners of all of the consumed coins.

If all of those conditions are met, then this PayCoins transaction is valid and Scrooge will accept it. He'll write it into the history by appending it to the block chain, after which everyone can see that this transaction has happened. It is only at this point that the participants can accept that the transaction has actually occurred. Until it is published, it might be preempted by a double-spending transaction even if it is otherwise valid by the first three conditions.

Coins in this system are immutable they are never changed, subdivided, or combined. Each coin is created, once, in one transaction and later consumed in some other transaction. But we can get the same effect as being able to subdivide or combine coins by using transactions. For example, to subdivide a coin, Alice create a new transaction that consumes that one coin, and then produces two new coins of the same total value. Those two new coins could be assigned back to her. So although coins are immutable in this system, it has all the flexibility of a system that didn't have immutable coins.

Now, we come to the core problem with ScroogeCoin. ScroogeCoin will work in the sense that people can see which coins are valid. It prevents double-spending, because everyone can look into the block chain and see that all of the transactions are valid and that every coin is consumed only once. But the problem is Scrooge — he has too much influence. He can't create fake transactions, because he can't forge other people's signatures. But he could stop endorsing transactions from some users, denying them service and making their coins unspendable. If Scrooge is greedy (as his cartoon namesake suggests) he could refuse to publish transactions unless they transfer some mandated transaction fee to him. Scrooge can also of course create as many new coins for himself as he wants. Or Scrooge could get bored of the whole system and stop updating the block chain completely.

The problem here is centralization. Although Scrooge is happy with this system, we, as users of it, might not be. While ScroogeCoin may seem like an unrealistic proposal, much of the early research on cryptosystems assumed there would indeed be some central trusted authority, typically referred to as a bank. After all, most real-world currencies do have a trusted issuer (typically a government mint) responsible for creating currency and determining which notes are valid. However, cryptocurrencies with a central authority largely failed to take off in practice. There are many reasons for this, but in hindsight it appears that it's difficult to get people to accept a cryptocurrency with a centralized authority.

Therefore, the central technical challenge that we need to solve in order to improve on ScroogeCoin and create a workable system is: can we descroogify the system? That is, can we get rid of that centralized Scrooge figure? Can we have a cryptocurrency that operates like ScroogeCoin in many ways, but doesn't have any central trusted authority?

To do that, we need to figure out how all users can agree upon a single published block chain as the history of which transactions have happened. They must all agree on which transactions are valid, and which transactions have actually occurred. They also need to be able to assign IDs to things in a decentralized way. Finally, the minting of new coins needs to be controlled in a decentralized way. If we can solve all of those problems, then we can build a currency that would be like ScroogeCoin but without a centralized party. In fact, this would be a system very much like Bitcoin.

Definition of Cryptocurrency

What exactly is cryptocurrency, how did it get its name, and how is it coded? Take a look at Coin Pursuit's plain-English definition of the term.

When you see the word root crypto in the English language, it comes from the Greek, meaning hidden or private. From it, we get words like encryption and decryption, which relate to the coding of a message, and its decoding once it's received. Even the English word crypt which uses the Greek root in its purest form refers to a private hiding place, a sanctuary for the remains of a loved one.

Cryptocurrency, then, means money that is made hidden and private and therefore secure by means of encryption, or coding. All aspects of cryptocurrency are protected by long and complicated blocks of code, each of which is unique to the item or person it's protecting. As an investor, or someone taking part in a transaction, you're identified by a one-of-a-kind code, as is the person or company with whom you're doing business.

Each coin of cryptocurrency itself has its own code, and smaller denominations have their own, as well, depending on what amount is needed for a transaction. Finally, the transaction itself is identified with its own code. Layer upon layer of encryption is one of the things that makes cryptocurrency unique, secure and anonymous, if you so choose. And all that coding and concealment is what gives cryptocurrency its apt name.

As is true in any technical field, the industry of cryptocurrency not only has its unique jargon, but often terms that have synonyms that are used interchangeably. Therefore, we'd like to clear the air on that specific point right here: when you see the terms digital currency or alternative currency here or in any other source, for that matter those are just additional terms for cryptocurrency. As a matter of fact, you'll more than likely see digital currency used more often, as it has a less-technical and more user- friendly feel to it.

Advantages over Traditional Money

What are the differences between cryptocurrency and regular bill-and-coin money? Coin Pursuit will take a close look at digital currency's advantages.

First and foremost, digital currencies, like Bitcoin for example, aren't linked directly to the laws, rules or regulations of any government, corporation or bank. The interest rates, fees and surcharges you may have to pay on your bank account or credit card in no way effect your cryptocurrency. As a matter of fact, at the heart of digital currency is a sense of rebellion against these fees, some of which are so deeply buried in fine print as to be considered hidden? Along those same lines, the rate of inflation that can potentially diminish the purchasing power of your government- issued legal tender (such as the US dollar) doesn't touch the value of any alternative currency you hold.

Digital currency affords its users complete anonymity. When you make a purchase with your ATM or credit card, your personal information your name, physical address and often other identifying data is attached to each and every transaction. Businesses, banks and governments can use this data to track you and take note of your purchases. In contrast, cryptocurrency transactions carry no personal information without your adding it yourself.

Accounts that hold traditional currency can be garnished or frozen completely; the latter means the holder of the account has no access to the funds in it. Since cryptocurrency exists outside the regulations and laws that allow this to happen, it's very rare for an investor to be rendered unable to access his coins though in certain situations in which illegal activity is proven to have taken place, it can happen.

Investor Experience Not Necessary

Interested in investing in cryptocurrency, but you're not a Wall Street wizard? Coin Pursuit takes a look at why that isn't necessarily an issue.

Digital currency can be an investment. Some people buy it so they can spend it just like traditional currency, but some make the investment in the hopes that it will ultimately be worth more than what they initially put into it that, by the way, is what we call a return on investment (ROI). Like any stock or commodity, wise investing will, over time, result in a higher ROI.

That isn't to say you need to be a financial wizard in order to invest in cryptocurrency. We've said it before, and we'll say it again: it's a young field, and everyone involved in it is still figuring out its twists and turns. What's nice is that you aren't by any means alone, and there's a healthy and growing support network of fellow investors who are more than happy to help you with any questions you might have.

Insights on a Young Industry

Cryptocurrency's been getting a lot of press lately, and has been the basis of a lot of rumors. Steps to help clear up some of those.

Alternative currencies are at the heart of a young and exciting new industry and as a result, they've gotten a lot of media attention. As you can imagine, some of that attention has been negative.

Since cryptocurrency transactions are anonymous, it's inevitable that some less-than-scrupulous characters will use them for illegal activities. There are several articles out there that discuss how digital currencies like Bitcoin and Litecoin have been used for drug trading and money laundering. Do we really need to point out that could happen with any financial tool you can name?

All types of currency have been used illegally throughout human history. Mob bosses like Al Capone and John Gotti laundered untold millions of dollars, and used a lot of that money for illegal purposes. British loyalists during the American Revolution destroyed new American currency to devalue it. Even back in Merrie Olde England, Robin Hood raided the royal treasury and distributed it among the poor. (Okay, it's true he's considered a hero, but under royal law it was illegal.) The point? Don't condemn digital currency overall just because a few bad apples are putting it to bad use. It's nothing new, nor is it unique to cryptocurrency.

The active cryptocurrency markets, and how some rise and fall rapidly. Turn the electronic page, and you'll find accounts of thefts of large amounts of digital currency from individuals and coin exchanges.

What Are the Business Benefits of Cryptocurrency?

In Merchants

In a recent article, strictly financial benefits of accepting digital currency as a mode of payment. While those are convincing arguments, there's a lot more to it than that. We'd like to take some time and look at the more socially-relevant, people aspects of using alternative currencies with your business.

Mutual Exposure.

When you sign on as a vendor with a particular type of cryptocurrency, both parties benefit from the arrangement. Issuers of the currency are eager and proud to publicly list the businesses that accept their product as a financial tool. Likewise, when you advertise in-store or on your company's web page that you accept a certain digital currency, it offers them more exposure. It's a win- win scenario for everyone involved, and can help boost the public status, reputation and legitimacy of both the digital currency and the vendor.

International Use.

Using credit cards or bank accounts for international transactions can be problematic; since they're linked to the legal tender of a specific government, exchange rates, interest rates, and country-to-country transaction fees can bog down the process and make it a lot more expensive, too. Cryptocurrencies aren't bound to the rules or status of any one government's currency, so international transactions tend to go a lot more quickly and smoothly when they're used. The Wall Street Journal recently quoted US Assistant Attorney General

Mythili Raman on the subject: The Department of Justice recognizes that many virtual currency systems offer legitimate financial services and have the potential to promote more efficient global commerce.

Less "Showrooming." As Techopedia puts it, show rooming occurs when a shopper visits a store to check out a product but then purchases the product online from home. Consumers get the best of both worlds; there's the in-store ability to physically check out the product, and the online advantage of buying it for less. There's nothing more frustrating to a business owner than to have a customer browse for an hour or so, and then make their purchase on their smartphone from a competitor often while they're still in the store! With the use of QR code scanning, and special discounts for customers who use digital currency merchants can use these tools as a way of cutting down on show rooming. The consumer gets a good deal, and the purchase stays in the store. Again, win- win.

Customer Anonymity.

Your credit, debit and ATM cards are all linked to your name, home address, and other unique personal information. As more media attention is being paid to the many ways personal info is being used without our knowledge or permission, consumers are starting to get annoyed by just how much is known about them by complete strangers. Merchants can track your purchases and know exactly what you eat, what movies you watch, what you wear, and so forth. For those who are saying, enough! Digital currency offers an alternative. All cryptocurrency transactions are secure, but they don't carry any personal information at all. This is a big selling point to folks who value their privacy.

No Surprise Fees or Waiting Periods.

Banks, credit card companies, and online payment services can delay certain transactions or apply surcharges and fees often without their customers knowing, unless they squint to read the fine print. This often winds up being bothersome and costly to both consumers and businesses. Cryptocurrencies carry smaller and more transparent transaction fees, and purchases and transfers can be approved in minutes.

Improving Reputation. Digital currencies had a rocky road to travel in the beginning, as drug dealers and money launderers took advantage of the inherent anonymity to make illegal transactions. The fact is, any financial tool can be abused, and cryptocurrencies are now gaining better reputations and a sense of legitimacy with both consumers and vendors.

Bloomberg Magazine quotes Jerry Brito, senior research fellow at George Mason University, on this topic: "like any new technology there are going to be some challenges. But they (US Congress) see there is a balance to be struck here and they are generally positive on the technology.

Trends & Disruptions

How can you Profit from Two Technologies, which are poised to disrupt the Largest Industry on the Planet? What is the Largest Industry? The Banking & Finance Market... An $80 Trillion (with a T) Dollar ($80,000,000,000,000.00) Market.

What if... You had, even a small piece of that Pie?

You need to wrap your mind around that. Imagine how this new technology could be protecting your family, while simultaneously, turning the entire banking system inside out.

You may be thinking, "Wow, What a Game Changer!" In reality though, it is creating a New Game, with new rules and new players.

This Once- in-a-Lifetime Opportunity is a game that Ordinary people, not just the Rich and Famous, can participate in.

With the entire Banking system on the verge of a disruptive change, are you seeing the massive potential to profit within this $80 Trillion Dollar Industry?

What are the **Two Technologies?

1. Smartphones
2. Peer-to-Peer Social Platforms

Do you understand the Power of this?

Everywhere you go, you see people on their Smartphones. What are they doing? Engaging with other people on Social Platforms! At their fingertips, they can be engaging in Facebook, Twitter, Instagram, Pinterest, Snapchat & Periscope, ALL within a few seconds of each other.

To be honest, we all do the same activities... It's Time to accept it and learn how we can Profit from it. The World & Technology are already changing at lightning speed. Can you keep up with it? Many people, in the financial know, believe the banking system is archaic and that we are way overdue for a technological disruption in the finance industry.

It is already happening. Take something simple, such as how the media handles their delivery of news. Do you remember when everyone bought and/or subscribed to their local newspaper? Now, Social Media Platforms have the Live Information on your screen way before the newspaper is even printed, never mind on the newsstands.

Quick Media Point... We, as Facebook users, are Media Creators. We post all types of content throughout our busy days and hurried lives, quickly & easily. Facebook doesn't create its content, We Do!

Are you seeing the 'Disruption Visual' a little more clearly? Paying close attention to Innovation & Trends as we head into our Futures, is of key importance, as they are moving forward fast, with or without us. There is a financial revolution happening right now, under our noses. It is driven by technology and will affect ALL of us.

Let's visit the Hospitality Industry for a few...

As an Illustration:

* Marriott International

    -4,000+ Hotels in 80+ Countries
    -Founded: 1957
    -Market Cap: $16+ Billion

* AIRBNB

  -Own 0 Hotels
  -Founded: 2008
  -Valuation: $25.5 Billion

This is Pretty Remarkable. If you haven't heard the AIRBNB Story yet, you need to read it as soon as possible. They have decentralized the Hotel Industry by creating a community marketplace where homeowners can earn money by allowing guests to book a spare space in their homes.

Another necessary Industry,

The Transportation Industry...

* U.S. TAXI Industry

  -Since the 17th century
  -Industry Size: $11 Billion Annually

* UBER

  -Founded: 2009
  -Valuation: $50 Billion

UBER decentralized the Transportation Industry by creating the Uber Mobile App, which allows consumers with Smartphones to submit a trip request, which is then routed to UBER drivers who use their own cars.

Do you agree that AIRBNB & UBER have disrupted their Industries? Not to mention, the early stage investors made up to 6,000% in returns.

Why Growing Numbers People Invest in Cryptocurrency?

Nowadays many people are deciding to invest in cryptocurrency. The reason behind this is that there is no required amount or papers to invest some of your money. Any amount will do for investment, unless you want to invest a bigger amount to have double or triple profit from it. Booming graphs of cryptocurrencies price attracts many individual to go for it.

Cryptocurrencies rise and drop from time to time – if you invested thousands at this very moment and have it back in millions in the next 4-5 years. There is also a possibility of losing the money you have invested so make sure to invest what you can lose.

Bitcoin, one of the most popular cryptocurrency in the world has driven many investors and traders in the past years. Many traders invest for this coin not just because it's the top crypto of the millennium, but because it is the most profitable one. If you are deciding to invest with this kind of industry, know the pros and cons first before doing so.

Advantages

Easy Access- Cryptocurrency is available in public and can be use by everyone. Investors all over the world can easily access because of the decentralized operation. Payment transactions has been made easy, while in a traditional payment system there is always a broker adding fees for every transaction you make.

Private- With cryptocurrency, you don't need to share your personal information or the details of every transaction between you and the beneficiary. All of the transactions are secured with the use of 'Cryptography'. Once a cryptocurrency transfer has been verified, it can't be reverses or charge-back, this protects the users from fraud and hacking.

Lower Fees- Unlike when using a credit card you need to pay for an interest, with cryptocurrency, charges and fees will never be a problem. All you need to do is make a research on what is the best wallet to use that matches the kind of cryptocurrency you are using. This can also be a major advantage for travelers.

Mobile Payments - If you are worrying about exposing all of your personal identification when purchasing online using your cards and bank accounts, well cryptocurrency just made it right for you. You can easy do payments and purchase to online stores without providing any personal information through the internet or recipient, only your wallet address will be visible to them. You can do all of these transactions using your mobile phone.

Disadvantage

Price Volatility- The volatility of cryptocurrency is the main disadvantage to be considered. Volatility is the risk level of the instrument where price is measured. So, investing in Bitcoin or any other online currencies is very risky, because the value of your money exchanged with them has no assurance. It can rise up to millions or maybe billions but it can also go to zero, no one can tell because no one controls it.

Possible Government Interface- The government cannot take your coins, but they can do such actions if they will decide to ban all those cryptocurrencies in a certain country. If the government will force online wallets and companies to shut down all your

Bitcoins etc. It will be frozen and it will be hard time to access them.

No Refunds- Refund is a No when using cryptocurrency especially Bitcoins – for instance you buy some product online and the merchant failed to deliver your purchased items, you cannot ask for a refund trough Bitcoins. Some cryptocurrencies such as Ripple have provided a chargeback option, but this will never exist on Bitcoins.

Best Cryptocurrency to Invest

1. Bitcoin- Despite of all the problem encountered by Bitcoin, it still remains as the number 1 choice for investing in cryptocurrency. With a market cap of $134 billion, Bitcoin still stand as the biggest cryptocurrency in the world. This cryptocurrency works as a store and payment system at the same time, letting users easily send and receive payments online. Bitcoin has been in the market for 9 years, and no one can easily break the weakness of this ingenious invention.

2. Ethereum- Ethereum has established itself as the second largest cryptocurrency in the world for the past couple of years. In fact, there are now millions of people who are holding this kind of virtual currency. The

ability of Ethereum to be second in the list can be its strength for raising a higher value in the near future.

3. Litecoin- This coin is one of the oldest cryptocurrency circulating in the market now. It has an advanced feature of security, storing data, and transaction time. Litecoin shows a beautiful growth like Bitcoin, no one knows maybe in a couple of years this cryptocurrency will draw a very high value in the market.

How Cryptocurrency Affects Our Daily Life?

In the past years of our lives we often do transactions in a traditional way of going to the physical store, bank, and payments outlet just to do so. But when that internet world provided the convenience, even sending money and buying goods can be done while at home in just a few click. Now, the paper bills and noisy coins also have their perfect version online, and its non-other than the cryptocurrency. This Virtual money have made us lazy, yeah this is true – many people are not contented using credit cards and debit cards when paying for goods and services online. They are now pushing the reality of using cryptocurrency with its feature of fast and anonymous peer-to-peer payment system. Some cannot just wait for hours to verify all of their transactions that is why they give cryptocurrency innovation a big try.

Did you know that some people also make cryptocurrency as a source of income? Yes, many people working at home have tried the trading and investment capability of online currency. As it gets profitable every second due to price hike, and all you need to do is watch over and monitor the graph rise and fall for your money. In general, cryptocurrency have built a virtual version of the actual money; lowering the fees and making every transaction as fast as lightning.

Can it change our lives?

Well, maybe if you invested such Bitcoins way back 2010, then probably you're a billionaire today. As a matter of fact, way back 2010, a programmer Laszlo Hanyecz offer 10,000 Bitcoins he'd mined in exchange of two boxes of pizza, what's more surprising about this is how rich you've think the seller of the pizza which was paid with Bitcoins. To tell you the truth, the pizzas are now 7 million dollars in price. So definitely it a big

YES on how cryptocurrency changes one's life.

Cryptocurrency lets people live with less hassle and long lines for payment transactions, and it could even make someone rich while just sitting and watching your investments grow. But some people tend to have bad experiences about this innovation, especially those who get scammed for buying such virtual coins online.

Characteristic of Cryptocurrency

Volatility- Cryptocurrencies value are very volatile, which means it has unstable value. Bitcoin is also prone to hacking, in 2014 Bitcoin price fell about by 23%.

Security- Most cryptocurrencies use wallets which are hardware and software that stores addresses for receiving virtual currencies. Wallets that are kept online with exchanges ability tend to be the prime targets of hackers. For a safer storage it is suggested to use an external hardware that can store all your precious coins with high security features.

Decentralized- A lot of cryptocurrencies are built-in with blockchain technology. This means that they are decentralized and run on several computers. Cryptocurrencies are not owned and controlled by anyone even the government has no involvement in this innovation. Both Ethereum and Bitcoin are equally decentralized, this is because of the concentration of the data and mining pools responsible for the hash capacity. Anyone who makes transaction and mine bitcoin and other currencies can actually be a part of the network.

Transparent- All the transactions and exchanges done into the network are visible anonymously in the blockchain ledger. Anyone can see what is happening with the virtual currencies especially the bitcoin. So if you have a bitcoin address, anyone will be able to see how much bitcoin is in your wallet.

Anonymous- Cryptocurrencies are considered anonymous, because of its feature that only wallet addresses are visible into the eye of the public. No one can even tell who owns a certain bitcoin wallet – the most anonymous virtual currency nowadays is the Monero, which is closely followed by Dash, Zcash, Vertcoin, Verge and Ether.

What Industry is next?

CryptoCurrency - A Digital Currency that is encrypted.

Prepare yourself for this next Great Technical Revolution... Never again will we experience a Financial Phenomenon like the One about to Impact All of Us. Are You Ready to Take Control of your Money?

"It is not the Strongest, nor the most Intelligent who will be the most Prosperous... It is the One who is the most Adaptable to Change." - C.D. & c.d.

"Where Can I Profit from This?"

Onward, why will Smartphones and Peer-to-Peer Social Platforms be so revolutionary within the Banking Industry?

1. Convenient
2. Decentralized
3. Faster, Less Expensive
4. Safe - Security & Verification

How are Fortunes Created? By Seeing Trends Before they happen. Smart & Wealthy People Follow Trends... See How Success Leaves Clues?

"Surround yourself with Only the People on the Same Mission as You, Who are going to lift you Higher & You Will Discover, 'Anything is Possible!'."

Are you aware that $99? Out of every $100 you are spending is digital currency? Whether you are paying by Credit or Debit cards, Electronic Check, paying online, using a Mobile App to pay for a cup of coffee... All are Digital Transactions. Yet, this Money involved in these transactions is not owned, managed or controlled by you, it is owned by Banks and Credit Card Companies.

What???

As a Result of this Disruption of Technology, We are moving from a world of Centralization to a world of Decentralization.

The very first Cryptocurrency was Bitcoin, established in 2009.

While Bitcoin has had its Success, It has also had some shortcomings and weaknesses. Taking this a step further... What if there was a way for ordinary people to still transact, still live their lives and still be able to move money around without going through the Banking System?

There is... A New Global Currency, positioned to be a key player and Dominant Force in the

Cryptocurrency Industry. We'll re-Visit this in a few...

"What would You Look for in a Cryptocurrency company?"

What you should Look for...

1. A Second Generation Cryptocurrency which has Instant Global Transactions. (Bitcoin has a delay in conversion to Global Currencies.)
2. Transactions will be Less Expensive than Traditional Banking methods. (Do you know how high the costs of transactions are with the current banking system? Credit card processing fees (2-3%) and wiring money ($20. - $60. +), Wow. Could that money better serve you, if it went into your pocket instead?)
3. It is designed to be controlled by you...to Protect, be 100% Safe and secure your Finances.
4. It has been Designed to handle High Volumes of e-Commerce, to the point where... If 100,000 people or 10 Million people started using it tomorrow, it will function without interruption.

5. It must be a Legitimate Cryptocurrency. We will be able to find it on Public Exchanges.

6. By using state of the art Technology, our Cryptocurrency Company will have its Own Instant Digital Payment Solution, making transactions Fast, Easy & Secure. It will be a payment solution provider with a 'Cash Back' program, Be Free for Customers to Download & Use, Offer a Merchant's Program which is offered for Free for Merchants, to be able to accept payments in our Cryptocurrency.

7. It will have the ability to convert our Cryptocurrency to US dollars, Euro, Yuan or any other Country's currency in real time transactions.

8. Merchant's Program must be Attractive for Companies, including...

-A Loyalty Program, FREE of Charge with No Monthly & No Set up Fees
-An easy, free download of the Merchant App
-Instant Verification of Payment
-Attraction of New Customers
-No Chargebacks
-No Fraud
-No Payment Processing Fees
-A Marketing Tool, Free of Charge

-Making Money from their Cryptocurrency Customers

9. Is designed to work Hand-in-Hand with Fiat Currency (paper money), not replace it.

10. For Customers...

-Their Mobile App will be Free & Easy to Use, Right on your Smartphone
-Have 'Peer-to-Peer' Secure, Instant Transactions
-Have Zero Transaction Fees
-No Limits on How Much or How Little Money to Send
-Instant Transactions, Globally
-Cashbacks and Discounts & a Loyalty Program.

11. Our Ideal company will also have an innovative Marketing Strategy in place, which will set itself apart from the masses.

12. It will have a Cryptocurrency 'Mining' company for its exclusive use.

Cryptocurrency Wallets Explained

What is a Cryptocurrency Wallet?

Before we start with what wallet you should use we better explain what exactly a cryptocurrency wallet is. A cryptocurrency wallet is basically a software program that enables users to send and receive digital currency as well as monitor their balance. The first step to using Bitcoin or any other cryptocurrency is getting a wallet.

How do they work?

Millions of people early to join the crypto movement currently use wallets however there seems to be a misunderstanding about how exactly they work. Unlike you 'pocket' wallet these digital wallets don't store currency. Actually, currencies don't get stored in any single location... or even exist anywhere in any physical form (brain explodes). All that exists is the transactions recorded and stored on the blockchain.

When a person sends through bitcoins or any other type of cryptocurrency to you they are basically signing off ownership of the coins to your wallet's address. Next, to be able to spend those coins and to access your money, the private key stored in your wallet must match the public address that the sender assigned it to. This does bring up one issue, if the address doesn't match, the coins are often lost forever. If it is a match your balance will increase and the senders will decrease by the amount that was transferred. All this means that there is no actual exchange of real coins. The transaction is merely a record on the blockchain by which both balances are adjusted accordingly.

Cryptocurrency Wallet Guide

Is there more than one type of wallet?

Yes there are, in-fact there are several types of wallets that provide different ways to access and store your digital currency. Wallets can be broken down into three main categories: desktop, software, hardware and paper.

Software wallets may be desktop, online or mobile.

Desktop wallets have to be downloaded and installed. They are accessible ONLY from the single computer that they are downloaded on. They offer one of the highest levels of security provided your computer isn't hacked or gets a virus because there is the possibility that you may lose all your funds.

Online wallets are accessible from any computing device at any location and are run exclusively on the cloud. While they are far more convenient to access they are after all controlled by a third party which makes them vulnerable to hacking attacks and theft.

Mobile wallets are run from an app on your phone and are useful because they can be used anywhere, for example, retail stores. Mobile wallets are usually smaller and simpler and definitely serve a purpose.

Hardware wallets are different to software wallets in that they store the user's private key offline on a hardware device such as a USB. Although these wallets make transactions online they are actually stored offline which makes them far more secure. Hardware wallets are compatible with a number of web interfaces. Hardware wallets make it possible to easily transact while at the same time keep your money offline and safe from danger.

Paper wallets are extremely easy to use and provide the highest level of security. While the term paper wallet doesn't exactly sound secure it refers to a physical copy or printout of your public and private keys. It is relatively straightforward to use a paper wallet. To transfer Bitcoin or any other currency to your paper wallet is done by the transfer of funds from your software wallet to the public address shown on your paper wallet. After the funds are transferred there is no way for anyone to access your funds without taking your piece of paper from you in person. If you wanted to spend your currency you would need to transfer the funds from your paper wallet to your software wallet and can be done by entering your private keys or by scanning the QR code on the paper wallet.

Are Cryptocurrency wallets secure?

The level of security depends on the type of wallet you use and the service provider. Intrinsically the web is a riskier environment to keep your currency compared to offline and can be exposed to the possible vulnerabilities in the wallet platform which can be exploited by hackers to steal your funds.

On the other hand offline wallets cannot be hacked simply because they aren't connected to an online network and don't rely on a third party for security.

Although online wallets have historically been the most prone to hacking attack it is of the utmost importance to follow diligent security precautions when using any wallet. Remember that no matter which wallet you use, losing your private keys will lead you to lose your money. SO DON'T MISPLACE YOUR PAPER. Transactions on the blockchain are not reversible so you must take precautions and be very careful!

Multi-currency or single use?

Recently, the biggest limitations to these wallets is that there actually isn't any available applications that can hold the range and variety of crypto currencies that are currently invested in. Although Bitcoin is the most well-known and popular digital currency there are so many alt coins out there. Alot of these wallets can support around 7-10 currencies which is a great start and since most of the new tokens are built on the Ethereum network they can be stored in your ETH wallet.

Are there any transaction fees?

That is a very difficult question to answer.

Transaction fees in the crypto space are a fraction of traditional bank fees. Sometimes there are fees that need to be paid for specific transactions to network miners as a processing fee while there are some transactions that don't have any fee whatsoever. It's also possible to set your own fee. As a guide, the median transaction size of 226 bytes would result in a fee of 18,080 satoshis or $0.12. In some cases, if you choose to set a low fee, your transaction may get low priority, and you might have to wait hours or even days for the transaction to get confirmed hence the downfall of choosing your own fees (surprise right).

In summation, fees are not an important aspect to think about when choosing which wallet you should use. You will either pay tiny transaction fees, choose the fee amount you are willing to pay or simply pay no fees at all.

CHAPTER FOUR

Are cryptocurrency wallets anonymous?

Kind of, but not really. Wallets are pseudonymous. While wallets aren't tied to the actual identity of a user, all transactions are stored publicly and permanently on the blockchain. Your name or personal street address won't be there, but data like your wallet address could be traced to your identity in a number of ways. While there are efforts underway to make anonymity and privacy easier to achieve, there are obvious downsides to full anonymity.

Which Cryptocurrency wallet is the best?

There is an ever-growing list of options. Before picking a wallet, you should, however, consider how you intend to use it.

Do you need a wallet for everyday purchases or just buying and holding digital currency for an investment?

Do you plan to use several currencies or one single currency?

Do you require access to your digital wallet from anywhere or only from home?

Take some time to assess your requirements and then choose the most suitable wallet for you.

Bread Wallet

Bread Wallet is a simple mobile Bitcoin digital wallet that makes sending bitcoins as easy as sending an email. The wallet can be downloaded from the App Store or Google Play. Bread Wallet offers a standalone client, so there is no server to use when sending or receiving bitcoins. That means users can access their money and are in full control of their funds at all times. Overall, Bread Wallet's clean interface, lightweight design and commitment to continually improve security, make the application safe, fast and a pleasure to use for both beginners and experienced users alike.

Pros: Good privacy & security, beginner friendly, simple & clean, open source software, free.

Cons: No web or desktop interface, lacks features, hot wallet.

Mycelium

Advanced users searching for a Bitcoin mobile digital wallet, should look no further than mycelium. The Mycelium mobile wallet allows iPhone and Android users to send and receive bitcoins and keep complete control over bitcoins. No third party can freeze or lose your funds! With enterprise-level security superior to most other apps and features like cold storage and encrypted PDF backups, an integrated QR-code scanner, a local trading marketplace and secure chat amongst others, you can understand why Mycelium has long been regarded as one of the best wallets on the market.

Pros: Good privacy, advanced security, feature rich, open source software, free

Cons: No web or desktop interface, hot wallet, not for beginners

Exodus

Exodus is a relatively new and unknown digital wallet that is currently only available on the desktop. It enables the storage and trading of Bitcoin, Ether, Litecoins, Dogecoins and Dash through an incredibly easy to use, intuitive and beautiful interface. Exodus also offers a very simple guide to backup your wallet. One of the great things about Exodus is that it has a built in shapeshift exchange that allows users to trade altcoins for bitcoins and vice versa without leaving the wallet.

Pros: Good privacy & security, beginner friendly, intuitive, easy to use, in-wallet trading, supports multiple currencies, open source software, free.

Cons: Hot wallet, no web interface or mobile app

Copay

Created by Bitpay, Copay is one of the best digital wallets on the market. If you're looking for convenience, Copay is easily accessed through a user-friendly interface on desktop, mobile or online. One of the best things about Copay is that it's a multi-signature wallet so friends or business partners can share funds. Overall, Copay has something for everyone. It's simple enough for entry-level users but has plenty of additional geeky features that will impress more experienced players as well.

Pros: Good privacy & security, multisig transactions, multiple platforms & devices, multiple wallet storage, beginner friendly, open source software, free

Cons: Can be slow & unresponsive, limited user support

Jaxx

Jaxx is a multi-currency Ether, Ether Classic, Dash, DAO, Litecoin, REP, Zcash, Rootstock, Bitcoin wallet and user interface. Jaxx has been designed to deliver a smooth Bitcoin and Ethereum experience. It is available on a variety of platforms and devices (Windows, Linux, Chrome, Firefox, OSX, Android mobile & tablet, iOS mobile & tablet) and connects with websites through Firefox and Chrome extensions. Jaxx allows in wallet conversion between Bitcoin, Ether and DAO tokens via Shapeshift and the import of Ethereum paper wallets. With an array of features and the continual integration of new currencies, Jaxx is an excellent choice for those who require a multi-currency wallet.

Pros: Good privacy & security, Multi-currency, wallet linking across multiple platforms, great user support, feature rich, user friendly, free.

Cons: Code is not open source, can be slow to load.

Armory

Armory is an open source Bitcoin desktop wallet perfect for experienced users that place emphasis on security. Some of Armory's features include cold storage, multi-signature transactions, one-time printable backups, multiple wallets interface, GPU-resistant wallet encryption, key importing, key sweeping and more. Although Armory takes a little while to understand and use to it's full potential, it's a great option for more tech savvy bitcoiners looking to keep their funds safe and secure.

Pros: Good privacy, great security features, multi-signature options, solid cold storage options, free.

Cons: Only accessible via the desktop client, not for beginners.

Trezor

Trezor is a hardware Bitcoin wallet that is ideal for storing large amounts of bitcoins. Trezor cannot be infected by malware and never exposes your private keys which make it as safe as holding traditional paper money. Trezor is open source and transparent, with all technical decisions benefiting from wider community consultation. It's easy to use, has an intuitive interface and is Windows, OS X and Linux friendly. One of the few downsides of the Trezor wallet is that it must be with you to send bitcoins. This, therefore, makes Trezor best for inactive savers, investors or people who want to keep large amounts of Bitcoin highly secure.

Pros: Good security & privacy, cold storage, easy to use a web interface, in-built screen, open source software, beginner friendly.

Cons: Costs $99, must have device to send bitcoins

Ledger Nano

The Ledger Wallet Nano is a new hierarchical deterministic multisig hardware wallet for bitcoin users that aims to eliminate a number of attack vectors through the use of a second security layer. This tech-heavy description does not mean much to the average consumer, though, describing what makes the Ledger Wallet Nano tick. In terms of hardware, the Ledger Wallet Nano is a compact USB device based on a smart card. It is roughly the size of a small flash drive, measuring 39 x 13 x 4mm (1.53 x 0.51 x 0.16in) and weighing in at just 5.9g.

Pros: Screen/device protected by metal swivel cover

Multi Currency support

3rd-Party apps can run from device

U2F support

When recovering wallet from seed, the whole process can be done from the device without even connecting it to a computer!

Fairly inexpensive (~$65 USD)

Cons: Not as advanced wallet software (no transaction labeling)

No ability to create hidden accounts

No password manager

Green Address

Green Address is a user-friendly Bitcoin wallet that's an excellent choice for beginners. Green Address is accessible via desktop, online or mobile with apps available for Chrome, iOS, and Android. Features include multi-signature addresses & two-factor authentications for enhanced security, paper wallet backup, and instant transaction confirmation. A downside is that Green Address is required to approve all payments, so you do not have full control over your spending.

Pros: Solid security, multi-platform & device, multi-sig, beginner-friendly, open source software, free.

Cons: Hot wallet, average privacy, the third party must approve payments.

Blockchain (dot) info

Blockchain is one of the most popular Bitcoin wallets. Accessing this wallet can be done from any browser or smartphone. Blockchain.info provides two different additional layers. For the browser version, users can enable two-factor authentication, while mobile users can activate a pin code requirement every time the wallet application is opened. Although your wallet will be stored online and all transactions will need to go through the company's servers, Blockchain.info does not have access to your private keys. Overall, this is a well-established company that is trusted throughout the Bitcoin community and makes for a solid wallet to keep your currency.

Pros: Good security, easy to use web & mobile interface, well-known & trusted company, beginner friendly, free.

Cons: Hot wallet, weak privacy, third party trust required, has experienced outages.

Cryptocurrency Exchanges

What is a cryptocurrency exchange?

An exchange is a website which facilitates the buying, selling and exchanging of cryptocurrencies for other digital currencies or more traditional currencies like the US dollar. For those interested in professional trading there are exchanges out there that host all the fancy trading tools however you will most likely need to verify your ID to open an account. If you are just interested in making the occasional, straightforward trade there are also platforms that you can use that do not require an account.

Different exchange types

Trading Platforms – Websites that connect buyers and sellers together. They take a cut of every trade facilitated by their platforms.

Direct Trading – These websites offer p2p trading and don't have a fixed market price, instead each seller sets their own price. These platforms are most commonly used by people wanting to avoid ID verification.

Brokers – Platforms like Coinbase that anyone can visit to buy cryptocurrencies at their price (usually updated every 10 seconds). This process is similar to using a foreign exchange dealer if you want to move your US dollars into Australian dollars for example.

Key points when picking your exchange, Like anything in the crypto space it is important to do your homework before you start trading. Here are a few things to check before making your first trade.

Reputation – The best way to find out about an exchange is to search through reviews from individual users and well-known industry websites. You can ask any questions you might have on forums like BitcoinTalk or Reddit.

Fees – Most exchanges should have fee-related information on their websites. Before joining, make sure you understand deposit, transaction and withdrawal fees. Fees can differ substantially depending on the exchange you use.

Payment Methods – What payment methods are available on the exchange? Credit & debit card? Wire transfer? PayPal? If an exchange has limited payment options then it may not be convenient for you to use it. Remember that purchasing cryptocurrencies with a credit card will always require identity verification and come with a premium price as there is a higher risk of fraud and higher transaction and processing fees. Purchasing cryptocurrency via wire transfer will take significantly longer as it takes time for banks to process.

Verification Requirements – The vast majority of the Bitcoin trading platforms both in the US and the UK require some sort of ID verification in order to make deposits & withdrawals. Some exchanges will allow you to remain anonymous. Although verification, which can take up to a few days, might seem like a pain, it protects the exchange against all kinds of scams and money laundering.

Geographical Restrictions – Some specific user functions offered by exchanges are only accessible from certain countries. Make sure the exchange you want to join allows full access to all platform tools and functions in the country you currently live in.

Exchange Rate – Different exchanges have different rates. You will be surprised how much you can save if you shop around. It's not uncommon for rates to fluctuate up to 10% and even higher in some instances.

The Best Cryptocurrency Exchanges

Today there are a host of platforms to choose from, but not all exchanges are created equal. This list is based on user reviews as well as a host of other criteria such as user-friendliness, accessibility, fees, and security. Here are ten of the best crypto exchanges in no specific order listed and explained by block geeks.

Coinbase

Backed by trusted investors and used by millions of customers globally, Coinbase is one of the most popular and well-known brokers and trading platforms in the world. The Coinbase platform makes it easy to securely buy, use, store and trade digital currency. Users can purchase bitcoins, Ether and now Litecoin from Coinbase through a digital wallet available on Android & iPhone or through trading with other users on the company's Global Digital Asset Exchange (GDAX) subsidiary. GDAX currently operates in the US, Europe, UK, Canada, Australia and Singapore. GDAX does not currently charge any transfer fees for moving funds between your Coinbase account and GDAX account. For now, the selection of tradable currencies will, however, depend on the country you live in. Check out the Coinbase FAQ and GDAX FAQ

Pros: Good reputation, security, reasonable fees, beginner friendly, stored currency is covered by Coinbase insurance.

Cons: Customer support, limited payment methods, limited countries supported, non-uniform rollout of services worldwide, GDAX suitable for technical traders only.

Kraken

Founded in 2011, Kraken is the largest Bitcoin exchange in euro volume and liquidity and is a partner in the first cryptocurrency bank. Kraken lets you buy and sell bitcoins and trade between bitcoins and euros, US Dollars, Canadian Dollars, British Pounds and Japanese Yen. It's also possible to trade digital currencies other than Bitcoin like Ethereum, Monero, Ethereum Classic, Augur REP tokens, ICONOMI, Zcash, Litecoin, Dogecoin, Ripple and Stellar/Lumens. For more experienced users, Kraken offers margin trading and a host of other trading features. Kraken is a great choice for more experienced traders. Check out the Kraken FAQ

Pros: Good reputation, decent exchange rates, low transaction fees, minimal deposit fees, feature rich, great user support, secure, supported worldwide.

Cons: Limited payment methods, not suitable for beginners, unintuitive user interface.

Cex.io

Cex.io provides a wide range of services for using bitcoin and other cryptocurrencies. The platform lets users easily trade fiat money with cryptocurrencies and conversely cryptocurrencies for fiat money. For those looking to trade bitcoins professionally, the platform offers personalized and user-friendly trading dashboards and margin trading. Alternatively, CEX also offers a brokerage service which provides novice traders an extremely simple way to buy bitcoin at prices that are more or less in line with the market rate. The Cex.io website is secure and intuitive and cryptocurrencies can be stored in safe cold storage. Check out the Cex.io FAQ

Pros: Good reputation, good mobile product, supports credit cards, beginner friendly, decent exchange rate, supported worldwide.

Cons: Average customer support, drawn out verification process, depositing is expensive.

ShapeShift

ShapeShift is the leading exchange that supports a variety of cryptocurrencies including Bitcoin, Ethereum, Monero, Zcash, Dash, Dogecoin and many others. Shapeshift is great for those who want to make instant straightforward trades without signing up to an account or relying on a platform to hold their funds. ShapeShift does not allow users to purchase crypto's with debit cards, credit cards or any other payment system. The platform has a no fiat policy and only allows for the exchange between bitcoin and the other supported cryptocurrencies. Visit the Shapeshift FAQ

Pros: Good reputation, beginner friendly, Dozens of Crypto's available for exchange, fast, reasonable prices.

Cons: Average mobile app, no fiat currencies, limited payment options and tools.

Poloniex

Founded in 2014, Poloniex is one of the world's leading cryptocurrency exchanges. The exchange offers a secure trading environment with more than 100 different Bitcoin cryptocurrency pairings and advanced tools and data analysis for advanced traders. As one of the most popular trading platforms with the highest trading volumes, users will always be able to close a trade position. Poloniex employs a volume-tiered, maker-taker fee schedule for all trades so fees are different depending on if you are the maker or the taker. For makers, fees range from 0 to 0.15%, depending on the amount traded.

For takers, fees range from 0.10 to 0.25%. There are no fees for withdrawals beyond the transaction fee required by the network. One of the unique tools on the Poloniex platform is the chat box which is constantly filled with user help and just about everything. Any user can write almost anything but inappropriate comments are eventually deleted by moderators. It can sometimes be hard to distinguish the good advice from the bad, but the Chatbox is a great tool that will keep you engaged.

Pros: fast account creation, feature rich, BTC lending, high volume trading, user-friendly, low trading fees, open API.

Cons: Slow customer service, no fiat support.

Bitstamp

Bitstamp is a European Union based bitcoin marketplace founded in 2011. The platform is one of the first generation bitcoin exchanges that has built up a loyal customer base. Bitstamp is well known and trusted throughout the bitcoin community as a safe platform. It offers advanced security features such as two-step authentication, multisig technology for its wallet and fully insured cold storage. Bitstamp has 24/7 support and a multilingual user interface and getting started is relatively easy. After opening a free account and making a deposit, users can start trading immediately. Check out the Bitstamp FAQ and the Fee Schedule

Pros: Good reputation, high-level security, worldwide availability, low transaction fees, good for large transactions.

Cons: Not beginner friendly, limited payment methods, high deposit fees, user interface.

CoinMama

CoinMama is a veteran broker platform that anyone can visit to buy bitcoin or Ether using your credit card or cash via MoneyGram and the Western Union.

CoinMama is great for those who want to make instant straightforward purchases of digital currency using their local currency. Although the CoinMama service is available worldwide, users should be aware that some countries may not be able to use all the functions of the site. CoinMama is available in English, German, French, Italian and Russian. Check out the CoinMama FAQ

Pros: Good reputation, beginner friendly, great user interface, good range of payment options, available worldwide, fast transaction time.

Cons: High exchange rates, a premium fee for credit card, no bitcoin sell function, average user support.

Bitsquare

Bitsquare is a user-friendly peer to peer exchange that allows you to buy and sell bitcoins in exchange for fiat currencies or cryptocurrencies. Bitsquare markets itself as a truly decentralized and peer to peer exchange that is instantly accessible and requires no need for registration or reliance on a central authority. Bitsquare never holds user funds and no one except trading partners exchange personal data. The platform offers great security with multisig addresses, security deposits and purpose built arbitrator system in case of trade disputes. If you want to remain anonymous and don't trust anyone, Bitsquare is the perfect platform for you. Check out the Bitsquare FAQ

Pros: Good reputation, secure & private, a vast amount of cryptocurrencies available, no sign-up, decent fees, open source, available worldwide, good for advanced traders.

Cons: Limited payment options, average customer support, more advancced.

The Ultimate Guide To The Best Cryptocurrency Exchanges

LocalBitcoin

LocalBitcoin is a P2P Bitcoin exchange with buyers and sellers in thousands of cities around the world. With LocalBitcoins, you can meet up with people in your local area and buy or sell bitcoins in cash, send money through PayPal, Skrill or Dwolla or arrange to deposit cash at a bank branch. LocalBitcoins only take a commission of 1% from the sellers who set their own exchange rates. To ensure trading is secure, LocalBitcoins takes a number of precautions. To start, the platform rates each trader with a reputation rank and publicly displays past activities. Also, once a trade is requested, the money is held on LocalBitcoins' escrow service. After the seller confirms the trade is completed the funds are released. If something does happen to go wrong, LocalBitcoins has a support and conflict resolution team to resolve conflicts between buyers and sellers. Check out LocalBitcoins FAQ

Pros: No ID required, beginner friendly, usually free, instant transfers, available worldwide.

Cons: Hard to buy large amounts of bitcoin, high exchanges rates.

Gemini

Co-founded by Tyler and Cameron Winklevoss, Gemini is a fully regulated licensed US Bitcoin and Ether exchange. That means Gemini's capital requirements and regulatory standards are similar to a bank. Also, all US dollar deposits are held at a FDIC-insured bank and the majority of digital currency is held in cold storage. Gemini trades in three currencies, US dollars, bitcoin, and ether, so the platform does not serve traders of the plethora of other cryptocurrencies. The exchange operates via a maker-taker fee schedule with discounts available for high volume traders. All deposits and withdrawals are free of charge. The platform is only fully available to customers in 42 US states, Canada, Hong Kong, Japan, Singapore, South Korea and the UK.

Pros: Security & Compliance, slick/minimalistic and user-friendly design, great analytics, high liquidity.

Cons: Limited currencies, small community, average customer support, limited worldwide availability, no margin trading.

CHAPTER FIVE

What Is An ICO?

Are ICO's the future of fundraising?

Recently the ICO market itself hit 1bln. It isn't hard to see how when some ICO's are raising 185m themselves (EOS I'm looking at you) which is IMO more money than a business ever needs at that early stage. If you want to search for the biggest trend in cypto today it is definitely Initial Coin Offerings (ICO's). The idea is not necessarily a new one, it is simply a presale of a cryptocurrency or token of a blockchain project. This guide will demonstrate an overview of ICO's as well as some past, current and future projects.

What is An Initial Coin Offering?

ICO is the abbreviation of Initial Coin Offering. Companies offer investores some units of their new cryptocurrency or token. Payments are made with Bitcoin or Ethereum 90% of the time. Recently this has put some pressure on the ETH price as people have to buy alot of ETH around ICO times and then the companies dump all that ETH on the market after the ICO finishes. Since 2013 ICO's have become the mainstream way to fund the development of new projects. The pre-created tokens can be easily sold and traded on exchanges (after the ICO finishes and the tokens are listed). The idea then is that there will be so much demand for the token that when you can sell it, you will make a profit.

Due to the rapid influx of new crypto projects built on the back of the Ethereum network ICO's are becoming more and more common and are arguably entering plague proportion where it is becoming ever increasingly difficult to separate the valuable ones from the scams and shills.

With this turn, ICO has become a tool that could revolutionize not just currency but the whole financial system. ICO token could become the securities and shares of tomorrow.

A history of ICO

In early 2013 Ripple Labs began the development of the Ripple payment system which was created around their 100 billion XRP tokens. The company then sold these tokens to fund the development of the Ripple platform.

Several other cryptocurrencies have been funded with ICO, for example, Lisk, which sold its coins for around $5mio in early 2016. Most prominent however is Ethereum. In mid-2014 the Ethereum Foundation sold ETH against 0.0005 Bitcoin each. With this, they receive nearly $20m, which at the time was one of the largest crowdfundings ever and serves as the capital base for the development of Ethereum.

Ethereum itself then unleashed the power of smart contracts and has enabled ICO's on its platform ever since.

Ethereum – The ICO Crowdfunding Machine

One of the fundamental uses of Ethereum's smart contract system is to create a token which can be exchanged on the Ethereum blockchain instead of Ether. The name of this contract is ERC#20. It quickly made

Ethereum a host for a very wide range of ICO's. Ethereum has since found itself the main platform for crowdfunding and fundraising for the next generation of crypto currencies.

For those of you that have already participated in an ICO by an ERC#20 token you will know that it is fantastically easy: You transfer ETH, put the copy of the contract in your wallet and almost magically the new token appears in your account and you are free to do with it what you will.

Examples for successful ICO on Ethereum are:

Augur

Melonport

Golem

ICONOMI

Singular DTV

First Blood

Digix DAO

If you want to assess Ethereum's market capitalization you should not only look at the market cap of Ether itself but also on the value of the token, which adds something like $300 Million to Ethereum's $4 Billion market cap.

Legality

The legal state of ICO's is somewhat debated. The tokens are sold not as a financial asset but as digital goods which is why they are often termed "crowd sales". In this case, in the majority of jurisdictions, the funding of an ICO is not regulated which means it is extremely easy to access right now. At the moment ICO's mostly happen in a gray area of the law however in the future it is highly likely that they will be regulated and this could have a number of negative effects for investors. It may bear financial or legal risk in addition to added cost and effort to comply with the regulations.

Profit, Loss and Scams

Assessing the potential profit or loss of an ICO has become one of the most important aspects of investing in cryptocurrency. ETH for example was sold at ICO: 0.0005 Bitcoin and today is worth 0.008 which is a profit of over 10,000 percent. Augur sold for around 0.005 bitcoin at ico and are 0.09. A gain in value between 100 and 500 percent is common for a successful ICO

Many ICO has been a lucky choice for investors. ETH, for example, was sold at 0.0005 Bitcoin and is worth today 0,05 BTC. Profit: 10,000 percent. Augur token (REP) were sold for around 0,005 each and are now traded at 0,01. The gain in value of 100 to 500 percent in Bitcoin is common for successful ICO.

There is of course another side. Many ICO's end with losses or at least 0 gains. Cryptocurrencies like IOTA or Omni did not hold their value after ICO. One of the biggest problems and risks of ICO's is the potential for scams and semi-scammers. They look like this:

Build a glossy website, write some blocks of bullshit, promise the greatest project/cryptocurrency ever. They then post the sale address and people are free to send in Bitcoin or ETH. That is why it is so so so important to always do your homework and due diligence on any ICO you are considering investing in.

So while there were many large and successful ICO's many small and shady ICO's did collect funds and delivered nothing at all.

The ICO market is currently still completely unregulated. Everybody should be aware, that this does imply not only large profits for investors, but also large losses.

The hottest ICO of Yesterday, Today and Tomorrow

Let's have a look what's going on of the market for ICO. In the past years, there have been a couple of wildly successful ICO.

Hot past Cryptocurrency ICO

Ripple

Ripple Labs created 100 billion XRP-token which serve as an anti-spam mechanism in the payment network Ripple, as you have to pay your network fees in XRP. The XRP are sold by Ripple Labs; their value doesn't move in a clear direction, while the trend is more downwards. It started with around 5,000 Satoshi, sometimes felt below 1,000 Satoshi, raised above 7,000 and finally fell again to a new low of 600 Satoshi, before again raising on 3,000.

Next

Next was a new gen cryptocurrency made in 2013. For a start, the 1 billion token were sold to early investors. With the ICO the developers only got a double digits amount of Bitcoins. Today the NXT token, however, are worth much more and Next has become a relatively successful and stable cryptocurrency.

Mastercoin

In 2013 Mastercoin announced to build a layer on top of Bitcoin and sold the Mastercoin-token to investors. The developers received around 10,000 Bitcoin, which have been worth $1mio at this time. Mastercoin token gained value some month later; some investors made huge profits. Later Mastercoin merged with Counterparty and Omni.

Ethereum

The largest ICO by now was made by Ethereum. With a presale of around 60mio ETH, the Ethereum Foundation raised around 31,500 Bitcoin. This event has become one of the biggest crowdfunding ever and the start of a wildly successful cryptocurrency. The investors of the ETH-presale profited massively.

Lisk

Based on BitShares, Lisk is a JavaScript written Blockchain which enables smart contracts on sidechains. Lisk sold the coins for Bitcoins and received around $5mio.

Hot past Ethereum token ICO

While most ICO in the past has been restricted to building a new cryptocurrency, the smart contracts of Ethereum enable startups also to use ICOs to fund development. Most of them are working with Ethereum itself and trick their presold token somehow in the process. Some examples:

Augur

The decentralized prediction market uses so-called REP-token to decide on the outcome of events. 80 percent of these tokens have been sold to fund the development and got the team more than $5m. Today all the token are worth more than $100m.

Golem

The Golem project aims to create a decentralized supercomputer, to which participants can contribute with their own computer and earn money by selling its power. Golem uses the Ethereum blockchain for smart contracts; the GNT token is needed to pay for the services. The ICO was restricted on 820,000,000 tokens, for which the developers received more than 10,000

BTC. Today the market share of Golem is beyond 50,000 BTC.

ICONOMI

Iconomi is a platform for the management of virtual assets. The ICN token is something like shares on the platform and should receive parts of the profits. The developers sold 85,000,000 token and got more than 17,000 BTC for it. Today it has a market capitalization of nearly 40,000 BTC.

First Blood

The Asian platform for decentralized sportsbet finished the ICO of its token in some seconds. Most of them have been bought by a Chinese exchange.

SingularDTV

SingularDTV wants to merge Ethereum, smart contracts and the production and stream of videos. With the ICO the platform raised more than 12,000 BTC. Today the whole tokens are worth around 40,000 BTC.

SingularDTV wants to merge Ethereum, smart contracts and the production and stream of videos. With the ICO the platform raised more than 12,000 BTC. Today the whole tokens are worth around 40,000 BTC.

The token of above ICO can be bought and traded on exchanges. Some additional ICO has just finish some time ago and prepare to release the newly created token on the Ethereum Blockchain. These are the following projects:

Melonport

Like Iconomi Melonport aims to develop a platform for the management of blockchain assets built upon Ethereum. The MLN token the developers sold will be needed to use the platform and have been sold or more than 2,000 BTC few month ago.

Qtum

This project wants to build a platform for the easy creation and use of blockchain based smart contracts. For this mission, it could raise more than 14,000 Bitcoin in an ICO.

Chrono Bank

The "uber of recruitment" intends to build a platform with its own currency for freelance projects. They sold 710,000 tokens for more than 4,000 Bitcoin.

Dfinity

Similar to Golem, Dfinity wants to build a decentralized platform for cloud computing. In its ICO it raised more than 3,000 Bitcoin.

BlockPay With "only" about 1,000

With "only" about 1,000 Bitcoin the ICO of BlockPay was one of the smaller ICOs. BlockPay is a startup building a payment processor for several cryptocurrencies.

With "only" about 1,000 Bitcoin the ICO of BlockPay was one of the smaller ICOs. BlockPay is a startup building a payment processor for several cryptocurrencies.

This are just examples. There are hundreds of further more or less successful ICO.

Things To Look Out For

Not every ICO is worth your money. Some just throw a couple of keywords in the air, something with blockchains, distributed platforms, smart contracts and so on, without having a real business plan or just the skills to realize the project. But some are really interesting. Good ICOs have presented months ahead, and the investment community looks forward to participating in it.

Cryptocurrency and ICO Investing

We cannot stress enough how important it is to do your due diligence and research the projects you are looking to invest in. To keep it as easy as possible for you we added our checklist to ensure we pick as many winners as possible.

Is the dev team high quality. Do they have a reputable history? There are 2 mains rules of investing. Rule 1: Don't loose money. Rule 2: Don't forget rule 1. With that in mind, can you trust the dev team with your money?

Are you investing with founders who have been involved in previous scams? If so, back off immediately. There is a chance the coins price might grow but there is an even higher chance that you will loose your money. It is never worth putting your capital at such risk. Remember rule number 1.

Does the project of interest have a long-term plan? There is a trend recently with new projects of launching their token before even releasing their whitepaper. Which to me is madness. Before investing you should read the projects yellow paper, and if you can't understand that, at least their whitepaper. What is the team trying to achieve? Do they have the means necessary to accomplish their goals and more importantly have they hit any historic milestones. If not, that is a very bad start. What are the timelines of the project and what are the milestones.

Does my coin seem a little bit too well-marketed with too little solid ground and ideas beneath its feet. So many ICO's these days have a pretty webpage and then they are shipped out to sell. No whitepaper, no data, no proof. Watch out for these: will they be able to deliver?

There will be tokens that you will want to hold forever and there will be tokens that you wish to flip when they hit the exchange or perhaps after they hit their first milestone. In this case make sure you set your timeframe or exit price to reduce the effect of emotions on your trade. Keep in mind that even though your token looks like it will land on the moon post ICO, if it goes over your exit price, sell. It probably will come crashing back to earth. Stick to your plan, watch your emotion and don't forget rule number 1.

Is this coin actually valuable in the real-world? Some coins may increase in price due to demand, marketing and hype however this trade might not be sustainable. For a coin to have long term growth it must have real-world use cases or it WILL NOT last. Look out for those coins that seem too much like a get-rich-quick scheme.

CHAPTER SIX

Mining

Why Start Mining?

Reasons to mine are numerous and varied. Your reasons may change over time as you learn about Bitcoin and follow its progress. It is helpful to understand others' motivations to be able to trust the Bitcoin network and the currency it supports.

Many people get started mining by a natural extension of something else they are already doing. For example, Bitcoin mining is similar to other grid computing projects that have grown because they are fun and provide an opportunity to cooperate with others in solving a big problem.

In the case of folding at Home, a distributed-computing project focused on studying protein folding, users contribute their computer processing power to increase scientist's ability to understand how proteins fold. Donors and teams compete and cooperate to see who can help the project the most. By mining bitcoins, you help to solve the problem of creating a currency and payment network that does not rely on a central issuing authority.

Those who are involved in technology are used to constant innovation and realize it is important to stay informed as new technologies emerge. Bitcoin is a new combination of several novel technologies (cryptography, peer-to-peer networks, and distributed databases) and some users mine bitcoins to help build experience with these technologies.

Since Bitcoin functions as a currency and mining can be operated as a business process, a large number of miners do it for profit. It is a tough business however because Bitcoin prices can fluctuate fairly widely and investment costs for a mining business can easily be in the tens of thousands of dollars. If you can operate efficiently, you may want to attempt to mine for profit but be sure to do your homework before making any big purchases.

Mining is a way to get bitcoins and this appeals to those who might want to obtain bitcoins steadily without using services such as exchanges or by selling any good they produce or service they perform as a profession.

Another motivation may be for anonymity. If you solve a block and are careful to connect to the Bitcoin network using Tor (The Onion Router), mining is a way to obtain bitcoins completely anonymously.

In addition to being a payment network, Bitcoin is a software project and there are many software projects that depend on the Bitcoin network for their own success. If your project depends on Bitcoin, you may want to contribute some hashing power to the network to increase, even in some small way, the chance of success.

There are probably more reasons still but the final reason we'll list here to mine bitcoins is if you depend on the Bitcoin network for international commerce and wish to see it as strong as possible.

What Is Mining?

Bitcoin is really three things. First it is a protocol (or set of rules) that defines how the network should operate. Second it is a software project that implements that protocol. Third it is a network of computers and devices running software that uses to protocol to create and manage the Bitcoin currency.

Mining is defined in the protocol, implemented in software, and is an essential function in managing the Bitcoin network. Mining verifies transactions, prevents double-spending, collects transaction fees and creates the money supply. Mining also protects the network by piling tons of processing power on top of past transactions.

Mining verifies transactions by evaluating them against the transactions that happened before. Transactions cannot spend bitcoins that do not exist or that were spent before. They must send bitcoins to valid addresses and adhere to every rule defined by the protocol.

With a frequency that is targeted at every 10 minutes, mining creates new blocks from the latest transactions and produces the amount of bitcoins defined by the current block reward (50 BTC until late 2012). Miners also verify blocks produced by other miners to allow the entire network to continue building on the blockchain.

Finding Valid Blocks

To find a valid block, the miner builds a list of recent transactions and calculates some summary information about the proposed block. This summary is combined with a number called a nonce to create a block header. The hash of the block header is then calculated and to see if it is small enough to win at the current difficulty. If not, the nonce is changed and the new hash is calculated and tested.

There is no way to create a valid block except by a brute force search. Brute force means the miner tries one nonce, then another, and another, repeating the process until it gets lucky. During that search, the miner cannot predict if the next nonce will give a smaller hash than the last.

Since it is a brute force process, the only way to increase your chances of winning are to increase the speed with which you can try nonce. The more processing power you have at your disposal, the faster you can search and the more likely you will be to find a winning block.

Once a valid block has been generated, it is broadcast to the network and quickly verified by the other nodes in the network. The difficulty of finding a winning number is adjusted every 2016 blocks so blocks are generated on average, every 10 minutes.

Creating New Bitcoins

When a miner finds a new block, it includes a new address to which new bitcoins and any transaction fees are to be awarded. This reward is the monetary incentive for people like you and me to run miners. If the conditions are right, you can put mining hardware to work, paying for your time and electricity and make a profit by selling the resulting bitcoins that you were awarded.

50 bitcoins are awarded to the miner who finds each block. This will continue until block 210,000 is found at which time the block reward will halve to 25 bitcoins. The reward will then halve again every 210,000 blocks thereafter. This means the number of Bitcoins ever created will top out at around 21 million (estimated to occur in near 2040).

Where do these bitcoins come from? They are literally created by the network as part of the Bitcoin protocol. This is the same process that created any bitcoins you will ever own or use.

Mining Hardware

Above, the term miner to describe a person who sets up mining computers, the computer hardware doing the mining, or the software that executes the logic required in mining. Hardware is the focus of this section.

As you know, some computers are faster than others. Computers can have faster or slower processors, more or less RAM, bigger and smaller hard drives, and so on. It is also true that some types of processor are better at mining than others. Since the testing of nonce is a very repetitive task, computer hardware that does repetitive things quickly works best for mining.

What is commonly referred to as the processor in a computer (the CPU) is a processor that is very good at switching tasks. Its parts are arranged in a way that helps the computer switch from playing video to messaging someone or showing a PDF. The CPU is optimized for task switching since that is how it spends most of its time.

On the other hand, a computer's GPU (graphics processing unit) is called upon to do simple operations, like draw a triangle, or shade a pixel, as many times per second as possible. It is internally arranged for this purpose which makes it much faster and more efficient for Bitcoin mining. In fact, we find that common video cards can out-perform common CPUs by 100x or more. Since you are competing with other miners, mining with anything less powerful than the top 10 or 20 video cards is quite inefficient.

The most recent development in Bitcoin mining is another processor called the FPGA (Field Programmable Gate Array). An FPGA is simply a highly programmable processor. FPGAs tend to be more expensive than CPUs and GPUs but they are also quite efficient in their use of electricity. Miners who are looking to operate where electricty is more expensive can invest more money up front to buy an FPGA miner and then pay less in ongoing electricity costs.

Mining Software

If you're mining with a GPU, you will need software to direct the hardware to mine Bitcoins. Software is available for Windows, Mac, and GNU/Linux. Much of this software is free and open source software that you can download and setup yourself or with a little help from someone online.

Once you have the software running, it will tell you how quickly it is mining. This is a number denoted in hashes per second with common speeds today in the mega-hashes or giga-hashes per second. A hash is a step toward testing a nonce and mega and giga mean million and billion respectively.

The goal is to get as many hashes completed by your hardware as possible per unit time. The best software for your hardware will help you do that. Good software gives a good hash rate but is also stable, meaning mining doesn't stop because of a glitch in the software.

After you've chosen mining software, there may also be specific settings you will use when you start the miner. These settings, which vary too much from machine to machine to list here, will help to obtain maximum performance from your miner. You can find settings for your GPU on the bitcoin wiki and forums.

Running your miner

When you're ready to mine, you'll start your miner. This may involve starting the same program multiple times if you have multiple GPUs or you may choose to use software that runs as a Live CD or Live USB boot disk that will take over the entire computer and manage the mining for you.

You'll want to check on your miner from time to time to be sure it is running and getting a good hash rate. This especially the case if you've done some of the more exotic tweaks to maximize your hashes per second. There are mobile apps and websites that can help you stay updated as to the status of your miner.

When you win a block, your bitcoin balance will increase by the amount of the block reward plus the transaction fees that were paid with any included transactions.

Running Multiple Miners

If you are inclined to invest more hardware and resources into mining bitcoins, is possible to connect multiple miners together on a network. To do this, you'll need some basic network equipment like a router and a computer to run bitcoind (the bitcoin daemon). You'll need to setup a user and password so the miners can all talk to the running instance of bitcoind. When a block is found by one of your miners, your bitcoind will contain the wallet with the key that signs the block and claims the block reward and fees.

Running multiple miners has power and heat implications that you'll want to consider. A high-end mining computer can use as much power as a toaster, iron or vacuum cleaner so if a circuit breaker trips you'll want to re-evaluate how your power is distributed on your wiring.

In regards to generated heat, this may be a nice byproduct on a cold winter night but on a hot day you'll want to have a way to remove heat from your space.

Overclocking

Computer processors have a speed at which they run called the clock speed. For modern processors this is stated in gigahertz. After a processor is manufactured it is tested to see how fast of a clock speed it can reliably support. Chips that are not stable at higher clock speeds are sold as lower speed models. Adventurous computer users have, for many years, been squeezing out more power from their processors by increasing the clock speed a technique called overclocking.

GPUs generally have a software tool that is used to change the clock speed of the processor as desired. GPUs also have a RAM clock speed that can be adjusted.

As we said before the goal is to get as many hashes calculated as possible per unit time.

We want to get a high hashrate but we also want stability. The problem with overclocking is that there is a limit to how much you can overclock your GPU without causing your miner to lock up or freeze. When locked up or frozen, the hash rate will drop to 0 or, in the case of a multi-GPU setup, a fraction of what it would be normally.

In regards to GPU RAM clock speed, this is often reduced in order to save electricity and help video cards run cooler at a given clock speed and resulting hash rate.

Solo Mining

Mining is a chance endeavor and the probability of winning a block within a given period of time can be calculated. Unfortunately for many systems, the time required to have a good chance at mining a block can be in the months or years.

If you have several machines running at high hash rates, you will find blocks more often and may be able to absorb the variation in the rate at which blocks are mined. On the other hand if you're running with a lower hash rate and can stand running longer in hopes of getting lucky, solo mining can still make sense. If you would prefer more certainty and evenness of payouts, you will want to mine in a pool which will be covered in the next section.

Pooled Mining

Winning a block will most likely be quite infrequent so mining pools were created as a way to even out the rewards. Those who join a mining pool cooperate to mine blocks as a group and when a block is solved by one of the members, the rewards are shared.

The amount going to each contributor takes into account their hashrate and time mining for the pool. Mining pool operators may take a percentage of the Bitcoins as payment for creating and running the pool. There are many pools to choose from and mining clients can be easily switched from one pool to another.

It is a good idea to join at least two pools in case the first one becomes unavailable for some period of time. Without a backup pool, your hashrate will effectively drop to zero until your pool becomes available again.

Managing Your Bitcoins

Whether you're mining solo or as part of a pool, with one computer or with many, eventually you will have some bitcoins. Once you get them it is important to handle them properly. Let's go over the wallet and how your Bitcoins are stored in practice.

When you run a Bitcoin client for the first time, it creates a Bitcoin wallet. The wallet contains your private keys, made of long blocks of random letters and numbers that are meant to be kept secret. These keys are what allows your Bitcoin client to spend and, you to effectively own, your bitcoins.

From each private key, a public key and corresponding Bitcoin address are created. When someone sends you some bitcoins, their Bitcoin client uses their private key to sign the bitcoins over to one of your addresses. This transaction is broadcast to the bitcoin network and later recorded in a block.

The important point to know here is that bitcoins aren't actually sent anywhere. They are instead assigned to addresses. To send bitcoins to yet another address the private key of the address that owns them will be required. This means you need to secure and backup your wallet to protect it against theft, virus attack, or loss due to hard drive failure or natural disaster.

The simplest way to back up your wallet is to use the backup feature of your Bitcoin program. If no such facility exists or you would like an additional backup, find your Bitcoin configuration folder and make a full backup of it. Be sure to have turned off your Bitcoin program however before making this copy.

Place this backup on one or more flash drives or CDs and put those somewhere safe. Depending on the number of Bitcoins you have, you may want to keep your backups in a safe or safe deposit box until they need to be used.

In regards to backup, it is a good idea to test the backup on another secure system. It is said that you do backup but what you really want is restore. So test your backups. Just be sure to test it on another system because some people have lost bitcoins by restoring a backup over a wallet that had private keys that were not in the backup.

Next is protection from online threats. This means keeping the wallet either offline or on a computer that is disconnected from the internet. If you'd like to have reasonable yet secure access to your Bitcoin wallet you can use a live CD with your computer to access and manipulate your bitcoins. The live CD would include all the software needed to handle bitcoins.

If you're going to be placing your backups where other people may be able to access them, you can use encryption. Once encrypted, a potential thief would need your password to be able to access the wallet file and steal your bitcoins. As an example, and there are many, a program like True crypt provides a simple way to encrypt one or more files on any drive or computer you wish. The latest version of the Bitcoin program from bitcoin.org also includes wallet encryption.

Using Bitcoins

Bitcoins are money and can be used as such. You can send them to friends to settle small debts. You can sell something or work for bitcoins. You can also buy products and services online with them. Currently there are hundreds of business that accept Bitcoin online and around the globe.

For business that only accept dollars, Euros, yen and other national currencies you will need to exchange your bitcoins. This can be done on one of the many online Bitcoin exchanges or by finding someone local who will to buy them from you.

To sell bitcoins on an exchange you would create an account with the exchange, send them your Bitcoins and place an order to sell.

Then when a corresponding buy order appears, your bitcoins will be traded for the currency you prefer. Then you'll need to get your money sent to you via a money transfer method that is compatible with Bitcoin.

One very important feature of Bitcoin is irreversibility. Once bitcoins are sent to an address, there is virtually no way to reverse the transaction. I hesitate to even say virtually because doing so requires either extremely fast timing or government-sized mining power. No credit card company or bank can get them back. The mathematics behind Bitcoin are very strong.

Bitcoin is therefore incompatible with financial services that allow payments to be disputed or "charged back". Notable examples include PayPal, credit card, check, and ACH. In the economy that grows around Bitcoin, refunds will need to be performed by the receiver of the funds and buyers will be wise to use escrow services with vendors they do not trust.

Accounting

At this time there isn't much in the way of Bitcoin portfolio tracking or Bitcoin-based accounting software. It is wise however until something good comes along, to save records of all your transactions. You will want to know how many bitcoins you have, how you got them, and in which wallets they are stored.

How Buying Just One Bitcoin Could Make You a Millionaire Fast!

Old World Finance is dead!

The banking and finance industry may not realise it yet, but with the advent of Bitcoin, their death-knell has already been sounded. During the next few years Bitcoin and its underlying Blockchain technology will disrupt the entire financial industry in ways we cannot yet fully understand or predict.

But what we do know, is that those who recognised the potential back in 2010 and invested in this nascent technology - when Bitcoin had its first market price of just 6 cents - have been handsomely rewarded for their foresight!

Just imagine if you had spent just $100 buying Bitcoin back in August 2010, when it was only 6 cents a piece. By the time it hit $6,000 you would have made 100,000 times your original investment, or $10 million dollars! And even more at the current price.

Turning $100 into $10,000,000 is mind-boggling for sure, especially in such a short time frame. But this is the very nature of disruptive technologies and the profit potential they represent. Now you may be thinking: "Oh, how I wish I knew about Bitcoin back then. I could have been a multimillionaire by now!"

Fortunately it's not too late to cash in on the ongoing financial revolution that is Bitcoin. So let me put my proposition to you plainly. If you were to purchase just one Bitcoin now, you could become a millionaire within the next few years. I can already hear you saying, "It can't be possible for Bitcoin to rise that much in price! The whole idea is too risky and based on too optimistic a scenario." - but hear me out.

Yes there is risk. No one knows for sure what Bitcoin will be worth in the future, but there are plenty of use-cases and scenarios that make such a prediction possible. And when it comes to risk you always have to look at the potential reward and consider if the risk is worth taking.

Risking the money to buy one Bitcoin would be well worth it, if a $1 million outcome is highly likely. So the question is, under what conditions could Bitcoin be worth as much as $1,000,000?

There's one condition that can state quite unequivocally, and that's the fact Bitcoin would need to reach a total market cap of around $16.5 trillion in order for a single Bitcoin to be worth $1 million - based on Bitcoin's maximum supply and estimated number of "lost" coins. Keep in mind that "market cap" is the total value of all bitcoins in circulation. So based on a realistic supply of 16.5 million bitcoins - 16.5 million times a $1 million price would equal a market cap of $16.5 trillion.

How Bitcoin Could Reach a $1 Trillion Market Cap

Predicting future prices must take into account the fact Bitcoin has a maximum supply of 21 million coins (minus lost ones), with each one divisible by 8 decimal places. This is the reason Bitcoin is often referred to as "Gold 2", meaning its scarcity drives up the price when demand rises. And why would demand rise? There are many reasons, including the following:

Currency Debasement: To fully grasp the scale of this you only need to remember what things used to cost when you were young. It's not that prices have risen since then, rather that money has become worthless. And when money loses value rapidly things can get out of hand, like in Venezuela where the population is being impoverished by hyperinflation.

Economic Crisis: There is plenty of evidence we are in for another economic shock in the not-too-distant future, which many commentators believe will make the 2008 financial crash look like a picnic. Whenever there has been a major crash in the past, people have always turned to gold as a safe haven. Bitcoin has already established a similar safe haven status.

Political Instability: The world we live in is increasingly fragile as the old order is being challenged and overturned at an increasing pace. Witness the turmoil caused by the UK's Brexit vote or the emergence of President Trump in the USA. Such political shocks cause nervousness and concern in global markets and once again drives money to safe havens.

World War: Nothing causes panic and mayhem in financial markets more than war. The danger we face today is the real possibility of a war breaking out between major nuclear armed nations. Such an event would have a massive impact on every single person on this planet and have a catastrophic effect on global markets. Bitcoin could surely rise.

War on Cash: It's an open secret that developed nations want to abolish cash. Their reasons include such things as being more efficient, fighting criminality and terrorism, and of course eliminating tax evasion. Trouble is, without cash the only place you can keep your money is in the bank! And while banks were considered trustworthy and safe in the past, this is no longer the case. As an alternative digital cash, Bitcoin's price will likely rise as a result.

All of the events listed above will cause people to seek a financial safe haven, which has traditionally been gold and silver. However Bitcoin, as "Gold 2", has many features that gold lacks, including being easily transportable, transferable online, easy to transact with, very secure with a high level of privacy, and of course the aforementioned store of value quality as a result of its strictly limited supply. As a result, Bitcoin's price would likely increase as a result of such events. And to get some idea as to how much, consider the following.

The total value of gold in the world is approximately $7.5 trillion, based on this data. That's a really big number, as a trillion is 1,000 billion and a billion is 1,000 million. So to write a trillion as a number requires 12 zeros - or 1,000,000,000,000.

If Bitcoin captured just 20% of the existing gold market, its market cap would be $1.5 trillion. Using the figure of 16.5 million bitcoins in circulation, the value of each one would be around $91,000. And if Bitcoin captured 50% of the gold market, then this safe haven use case alone could drive the price up to around $227,500.

The truth is, there are multiple use-cases for Bitcoin and a gold-like safe haven asset is just one of them. For consider the following:

Global Remittances: This is a big one and ripe for full-on Bitcoin adoption. The total value of global remittances - people sending money back to their home country - is $585 billion per year. The top four countries for global remittance volume are China at $54.9 billion, the Philippines at $26.7 billion, France at $23.3 billion, and Mexico at $23 billion.

Global Unbanked: There are 2.5 billion people on this planet who are "unbanked", without access to traditional financial services. But they virtually all have mobile phones! Technology can enable such people to leapfrog over the "old" banking industry and adopt Bitcoin, giving them immediate access to the whole world.

Global Gambling: This is another perfect "fit" for Bitcoin, due to the difficulty those in the gambling businesses have with traditional financial services. The global legal market alone is estimated to be $700 billion a year, while the illegal market, including sports betting, is up to a staggering $3 trillion!

Global Drugs Market: One of the obvious consequences of drug prohibition policy in most countries of the world is the massive illegal drugs market, which has an estimated value of $4 trillion - a huge number. Once again, Bitcoin offers users an alternative and more private way to pay for it all.

Global Offshore Banking: A good portion of the world's private wealth is held in offshore bank accounts, with estimates of as much as $21 trillion on deposit. If half this money were to move into Bitcoin - due to increased pressure from governments to close down the offshore banking industry - then this amount of money alone, moving into Bitcoin, would result in a price of around $636,000.

While some of the above global markets may be unsavoury to many people, one cannot ignore the fact they exist and that Bitcoin could become the currency of choice for many of the people involved - pushing demand for Bitcoin even higher.

When you do the numbers on both "safe haven" and the additional use cases above, it's not hard to imagine the future value of Bitcoin being $1 million. But apart from that, more and more people are becoming involved in Bitcoin for a variety of valid reasons - including for financial privacy, investment and the potential of a truly global non-government currency.

Whatever the reason, ordinary folk are moving into Bitcoin at an ever-increasing rate. And at some point in the future this gradual migration to "better money" could turn into a stampede towards mass adoption! When that happens, all current future price estimates for Bitcoin could fall short.

If you add up all the quoted values of the different global markets listed here, you will soon realise Bitcoin can indeed become a major financial force, with a price far in excess of what we see today. So even though many people think they have "missed the boat" and that Bitcoin is already too expensive, the truth is they haven't, and it isn't! And here's another compelling reason why...

The Elephant in the Room

Ever since Bitcoin was unleashed on the world back in January 2009, when Satoshi Nakamoto mined the first "genesis" block, it has primarily been the domain of computer geeks, libertarians and assorted visionaries. In the past couple of years a new type of person has been attracted to the space - the speculator and investor, drawn by the extraordinary profit potential of this "new money" and asset class.

However, all such early adopters have mostly been individuals - people making the decision to invest and risk their own money in Bitcoin. But that is changing. In fact, we are about to witness an historic occurrence - the arrival of BIG money, the institutional investors.

The reason they haven't joined the party so far is because they haven't been able to - due to the lack of the suitable structures. Institutional investors require a properly regulated market in order to invest their client's funds. This includes being able to invest through licensed and regulated exchanges and having access to regulated custodial accounts. Up until recently these things were missing from the Bitcoin ecosystem. Not anymore.

You may be thinking, "Why would institutional investors want to risk funds in Bitcoin when it's so volatile?" The answer is simple. Firstly, more and more people want exposure to Bitcoin and its potential upside, and investment funds are responding to their clients' requests. Secondly, institutional investors are always interested in any non-correlated asset - which Bitcoin is. While global news, wars, market updates and changes in political leadership can spook traditional markets, Bitcoin has proven to be unaffected by such happenings - making it an ideal hedge against such, something all institutional investors are interested in.

2018 is the year institutional money arrives. Big money means exactly that - literally trillions of dollars sloshing around the world, looking for somewhere to park and profit. This new money coming into Bitcoin, with its strictly limited supply, can only do one thing - push the price higher. Many analysts are saying Bitcoin could rise up to 10x in 2018 alone - but this is only the start. It's also an historically unique opportunity to benefit from such an event.

The Million Dollar Question

So the question you should be seriously asking yourself is, "How can I get a piece of this action and give myself a fighting chance of becoming a millionaire?"

The answer is simple. Make it your goal to own one Bitcoin - just one. Then hold on to it for the next few years. Simply forget about it and get on with your life. If Bitcoin reaches its potential, as outlined here, then a $1 million price point is certainly possible. And if that's the case, you will become a millionaire just buy holding on to that one Bitcoin!

But what if it doesn't reach $1 million? Of course that is a possibility as no one can predict the future. But if you study Bitcoin's price history since its inception, you will note it has constantly risen over the longer term. Would you complain if it only reached $500,000, or even less like $250,000?

So that's my considered advice, to buy and hold one Bitcoin. However, if buying it seems daunting to you and you'd like some help, or you want more information about this whole crypto space - before putting your money down for one Bitcoin.

It's a comprehensive, step-by-step educational resource that's delivered in both video and text format. So if you're looking for a helping hand and guidance on how to buy, store, trade, spend and sell Bitcoin, then it could be just what you're looking for. More importantly, it will give you the confidence and knowledge you need to make an informed decision to buy Bitcoin - the one Bitcoin that could make you a millionaire within the next few years.

Start investing!

After engaging in your due diligence, it's time for you to finally purchase the coins that you're confident has the right fundamentals. In order to buy coins, you have to open exchange accounts. However, it can be tricky to find the right exchange since there are many things to look out for. Therefore, we've made it easier for you to choose which exchange is best for you!

Opening an Exchange Account

If you're new to cryptocurrencies, your first step would be to find an exchange that allows you to deposit money. Due to regulations, all exchanges require you to verify your account before depositing your funds, through the submission of your identity proof and any other personal information. Hence, you should find an exchange in your domestic country first to convert money from your bank account into Bitcoin.

It is important to note that not all crypto exchanges accept fiat money; some exchanges only allow you to deposit coins (most commonly Bitcoin) to purchase other alternative coins. Bitcoin is the most popular crypto that is offered on almost all crypto exchanges, and represents the gateway to purchasing other coins. In other words, if you want buy any other coins, you must do the following:

Step 1: Open a domestic cryptocurrency exchange in your country and verify your account (submit identity proof)

Step 2: Deposit funds from your bank account to your crypto exchange account and start buying Bitcoin

Step 3: Open a crypto exchange account that offers a variety of other coin. Usually these exchanges do not accept fiat deposits and only allows coin deposits.

Step 4: After verifying your account, transfer the Bitcoin that you've bought from your local exchange to your new crypto exchange and you can start buying other coins with your Bitcoin.

CHAPTER SEVEN

Consensus in Bitcoin

Consensus in Bitcoin, that is, the way that the operation of Bitcoin relies on the formation of consensus amongst people. There are three kinds of consensus that have to operate for Bitcoin to be successful.

1. *Consensus about rules.* By rules we mean things like what makes a transaction valid, what makes a block valid, and how the nodes in the peer-to-peer network should behave how they should interact with each other, the communication protocol they should use, and more generally all the protocols and data formats that are involved in making Bitcoin work.

You need to have a consensus about these things so that all the different participants in the system can talk to each other and agree on what's happening.

2. *Consensus about history.* That is, consensus about what's in and what isn't in the block chain, and therefore a consensus about which transactions have occurred. Once you have that, what follows is a consensus about which coins which unspent outputs exist and who owns them.

This consensus results from the processes we've looked at in earlier chapters from which the block chain is built and by which nodes come to consensus about the contents of the block chain. This is the most familiar and most technically intricate kind of consensus in Bitcoin.

3. *Consensus that coins are valuable.* The third form of consensus is the general agreement that bitcoins are valuable, that bitcoins are a good thing to have, and in particular the consensus that if someone gives you a bitcoin today, then tomorrow you will be able to redeem or trade that for something of value.

Any currency needs this whether it's a fiat currency like the dollar or cryptocurrency like Bitcoin, you need a consensus that the thing has value. That is, you need people to generally accept that it's exchangeable for something of value, now and in the future. In a fiat currency, this is the only kind of consensus, whereas in cryptocurrencies we additionally have the first two.

In Bitcoin, this form of consensus, unlike the others, is a bit circular. In other words, my belief that the bitcoins I'm receiving today are of value depends on my expectation that tomorrow other people will believe the same thing. So consensus on value relies on believing that consensus on value will continue. This is sometimes called the Tinkerbell effect by analogy to Peter Pan where it's said that Tinker Bell exists because you believe in her.

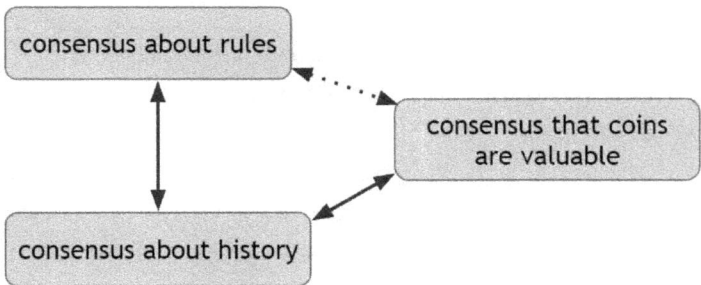

First of all, consensus about rules and consensus about history go together. Without knowing which blocks are valid you can't have consensus about the block chain. And without consensus about which blocks are in the block chain, you can't know if a transaction is valid or if it's trying to spend an already-spent output.

Consensus about history and consensus that coins are valuable are also tied together. The genius in Bitcoin's original design was in recognizing that it would be very difficult to get any one of these types of consensus by itself. Consensus about the rules in a worldwide decentralized environment where there's no notion of identity isn't the kind of thing that's likely to happen.

Consensus about a history, similarly, is a very difficult distributed data structure problem which is not likely to be solvable on its own. And a consensus that some kind of cryptocurrency has value is also very difficult to achieve. What the design of Bitcoin and the continued operation of Bitcoin shows is that even if you can't build any one of these forms of consensus by itself you can somehow stand up all three of them together, and get them to operate in an interdependent way. So when we talk about how things operate in the Bitcoin community we have to bear in mind that Bitcoin relies on agreement by the participants, and that consensus is a fragile and interdependent thing.

Bitcoin Core Software

The Bitcoin Core software is a piece of open-source software which is a focal point for discussion and debate about Bitcoin's rules.

Bitcoin Core is licensed under the MIT license which is a very permissive open-source license. It allows the software to be used for almost any purpose as long as the source is attributed and the MIT license is not stripped out. Bitcoin Core is the most widely used Bitcoin software, and even those who don't use it tend to look to it to define what the rules are. That is, people building alternative Bitcoin software typically try to mimic the rule-defining parts of the Bitcoin Core software, the parts that check validity of transactions and blocks.

Bitcoin Core is the de-facto rulebook of Bitcoin. If you want to know what's valid in Bitcoin, the Bitcoin Core software or explanations of it is where to look.

Bitcoin Improvement Proposals. Anyone can contribute technical improvements via "pull requests" to Bitcoin Core, a familiar process in the world of open-source software. For more substantial changes, especially protocol modifications, there is a process called Bitcoin Improvement Proposals or BIPs. These are formal proposals for changes to Bitcoin. Typically a BIP will include a technical specification for a proposed change as well as a rationale for it. So if you have an idea for how to improve Bitcoin by making some technical change, you're encouraged to write up one of these documents and to publish it as part of the Bitcoin Improvement Proposal series, and that will then kick off a discussion in the community about what to do. While the formal process is open to anyone, there's a learning curve for participation like any open-source project.

BIPs are published in a numbered series. Each one has a champion, that is, an author who evangelizes in favor of it, coordinates discussion and tries to build a consensus within the community in favor of going forward with or implementing a particular proposal.

What we said above applies to proposals to change the technology. There are also some BIPs that are purely informational and exist just to tell people things that they might not otherwise know, or that are process oriented, that talk about how things should be decided in the Bitcoin community.

Bitcoin Core developers. To understand the role of the Bitcoin Core software we also have to understand the role of Bitcoin Core developers. The original code was written by Satoshi Nakamoto, who we'll return to later in the chapter. Nakamoto is no longer active, but instead there are a group of developers who maintain Bitcoin Core. As of early 2015 there are five: Gavin Andresen, Jeff Garzik, Gregory Maxwell, Wladimir J. van der Laan, and Pieter Wuille. The Core developers lead the effort to continue development of the software and are in charge of which code gets pushed into new versions of Bitcoin Core.

How powerful are these people? In one sense they're very powerful, because one could argue that any the rule changes to the code that they make will get shipped in Bitcoin Core and will be followed by default. These are the people who hold the pen that can write things into the de-facto rulebook of Bitcoin. In another sense, they're not powerful at all. Because it's open-source software, anyone can copy it and modify it, in other words, fork the software at any time, and so if the lead developers start behaving in a way that the community doesn't like, and strongly rejects, the community can go in a different direction.

One way of thinking about this is to say that the lead developers are leading the parade. They're out in front of the parade marching and the parade will generally follow them when they turn a corner, but if they try to lead the parade into an action that disastrous, then the parade members marching behind them might decide to go in a different direction. They can urge people on, and as long as they seem to be behaving reasonably, the group will probably follow them, but they don't have formal power to force people to follow them if they take the system in a technical direction that the community doesn't like.

Let's think about what you as a user of a system can do if you don't like the way the rules are going or the way it's being run, and compare it to a centralized currency like a fiat currency. In a centralized currency if you don't like what going on you has a right to exit, that is, you can stop using it. First you'd have to try and sell any currency you hold. Just like almost any business that you deal with, you have the ability to just stop dealing with them if you don't like what they're doing. On the other hand, if it's a currency and you've got a lot of business, you've got a lot of assets tied up in it and it might be expensive or difficult to actually exit. Whether or not it's easy, with a centralized currency that's really your only option.

With Bitcoin, while you certainly have the right to exit, because it operates in an open-source way, you additionally have the right to fork the rules. That means you, and some of your friends and colleagues can decide that you would rather live under a different rule set, and you can fork the rules and go a different direction from the lead developers. The right to fork this is more empowering for users than the right to exit, and therefore the community has more power in a system like Bitcoin which is open source than it would in a purely centralized system. So although the lead developers might look like a centralized entity controlling things, in fact they don't have the power that a purely centralized manager or software owner would have.

Forks in the rules.

One way to fork the software and the rules is to start a new block chain with a new genesis block. This is popular option for creating altcoins, and we'll discuss altcoins in Chapter 10. But for now let's consider a different type of fork in the rules, one in which those who fork decide to fork the block chain as well.

At the point when there's a disagreement about the rules, there will be a fork in the block chain, resulting in two branches. One branch is valid under rule set A but invalid under rule set B, and vice versa. Once the miners operating under the two rule sets separate they can't come back together because each branch will contain transactions or blocks that's invalid according to the other rule set.

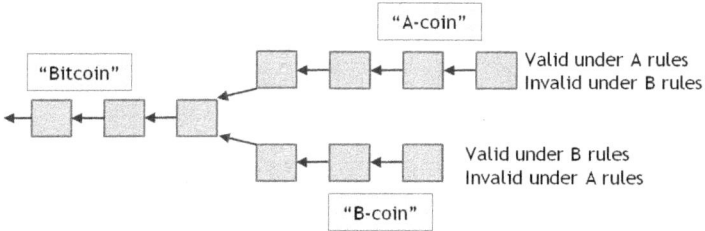

We can think of the currency we had up until the fork as being Bitcoin, the big happy Bitcoin that everyone agreed on. After the fork it's as if there are two new currencies which we can think of as being A-coin corresponding rule set A and B-coin corresponding to rule set B. At the moment of the fork, it's as if everyone who owned one Bitcoin receives one A-coin and one B-coin. From that point on, A-coin and B-coin will operate separately as if they were separate currencies, and they might operate independently. The two groups might continue to evolve their rules in different ways.

We should emphasize that it's not just the software, or the rules, or the software implementing the rules that forked, it's the currency itself that forked. This is an interesting thing that can happen in a cryptocurrency that couldn't happen in a traditional currency where the option of forking is not available to users. To our knowledge, neither Bitcoin nor any altcoin has ever forked in this way, but it's a fascinating possibility.

How might people respond to a fork like this? It depends on why the fork happened. The first case is where the fork was not intended as a disagreement about the rules, but instead as a way of starting an altcoin. Someone might start an altcoin by forking Bitcoin's block chain if they want to start with a ruleset that's very close to Bitcoin's. This doesn't really pose a problem for the community. The altcoin goes its separate way, the branches coexist peacefully, and some people will prefer to use bitcoins while others will prefer the altcoin. But as we said earlier, as far as we know, no one's ever started an altcoin by forking Bitcoin's or another existing altcoin's block chain. They've always started with a new genesis block.

The interesting case is if the fork reflected a fight between two groups about what the future of Bitcoin should be in other words, a rebellion within the Bitcoin community where a sub-group decides to break off and decides they have a better idea about how the system should be run. In that case, the two branches are rivals and will fight for market share. A-coin and there's a B-coin will each try to get more merchants to accept it and more people to buy it. Each will want to be perceived as the "real Bitcoin." There may be a public-relations fight where each claims legitimacy and portrays the other as a weird splinter group.

The probable outcome is that one branch will eventually win and the other will melt away. These sorts of competitions tend to tip in one direction. Once one of the two gets seen as more legitimate and obtains a bigger market share, the network effect will prevail and the other becomes a niche currency and will eventually fall away. The rule set and the governance structure of the winner will become the de-facto rule set and governance structure of Bitcoin.

Governments Notice Bitcoin

The rest of chapter is about governments, government interaction with Bitcoin and attempts to regulate Bitcoin. Let's start with the moment when governments noticed Bitcoin, that is, when Bitcoin became big enough as a phenomenon that government started to worry about the impact it might have and how to react to it.

Capital control.

One reason why governments would notice a digital currency like Bitcoin is that untraceable digital cash, if it exists, defeats capital controls. Capital controls are rules or laws that a country has in place that are designed to prevent the flow of value, of capital, of wealth, either in or out of the country. By putting controls on banks, investments, and so on, the country can try to prevent these flows.

Bitcoin is a very easy way, under some circumstances, to defeat capital controls. Someone can simply buy bitcoins with capital inside the country, transmit those bitcoins outside the country electronically, and then trade them for capital or wealth outside the country. That would let them move capital or wealth from inside to outside and similarly they can move capital from outside to inside. Because wealth in this electronic form can move so easily across borders and can't really be controlled, a government that wants to enforce capital controls in a world with Bitcoin has to try to disconnect the Bitcoin world from the local fiat currency banking system. That would make it infeasible for someone to turn large amounts of local currency into Bitcoin, or large amounts of Bitcoin into local currency. We do see countries trying to beef up or protect their capital controls to do that, China being a notable example. China has engaged in increasingly strong measures to try to disconnect bitcoins from the Chinese fiat currency banking system.

Crime

Another reason governments might worry about untraceable digital cash is that it makes certain kinds of crimes easier in particular, crimes like kidnapping and extortion that involve the payment of a ransom or payoff. Those crimes become easier when payment can be done at a distance and anonymously.

Law enforcement against kidnappers, for example, often has relied upon exploiting the hand-off of money from the victim or the victim's family to the criminals. When that can be done by email and at a distance in an anonymous way, it becomes much harder for law enforcement to follow the money. Another example: the "CryptoLocker" malware encrypts victims' files and demands ransom in Bitcoin (or other types of electronic money) to decrypt them. So the crime and the payment are both carried out at a distance. Similarly, tax evasion becomes easier when it's easier for people to move money around and to engage in transactions that are not easily tied to a particular individual or identity. Finally, the sale of illegal items becomes potentially easier when the transfer of funds can happen at a distance and without needing to go through a regulated institution.

Silk Road.

A good example of that is Silk Road, which was essentially the eBay for illegal drugs. It calls itself an anonymous marketplace. Illegal drugs were the primary things for sale, with a smattering of other categories that you can see on the left. It was the largest online market for illegal drugs.

Silk Road allowed sellers to advertise goods for sale and buyers to buy them. The goods were delivered typically through the mail or through shipment services and payment was made in bitcoins.

Silk Road held the bitcoins in escrow while the goods were shipped. There was an innovative escrow system which helped protect the buyers and sellers against cheating by other parties. The bitcoins would be released once the buyer certified that the goods had arrived.

There was also an eBay-like reputation system that allowed buyers and sellers to get reputations for following through on their deals, and by using that reputation system Silk Road was able to give the market participants an incentive to play by the rules. So, Silk Road was innovative among criminal markets in finding ways of enforcing the rules of the criminal market at a distance, which is something that criminal markets in the past have had difficulty doing.

Silk Road was run by a person who called himself Dread Pirate Roberts obviously a pseudonym, and you might recognize the reference. It operated from February 2011 until October 2013. Silk Road was shut down after the arrest of its operator Ross Ulbricht. Ulbricht had tried to cover his tracks by operating pseudonymous accounts and by using Tor, anonymous remailers, and so on. The government was nevertheless able to connect the dots and connect him to Silk Road activity to the servers and the bitcoins he controlled as the operator of Silk Road. He was convicted of various crimes relating to operating Silk Road. He was also charged with attempted murder for hire, although fortunately he was bad at it and nobody actually got killed.

In the course of taking down Silk Road, the FBI seized about 174,000 bitcoins, worth over $30 million at the time. As with the proceeds of any crime under US law, they could be seized by the government. Later the government auctioned off a portion of the seized bitcoins.

ssons from Silk Road.

There are several lessons from Silk Road and from the encounter between law enforcement and Ulbricht. First it's pretty hard to keep the real world and the virtual world separate. Ulbricht believed that he could live his real life in society and at the same time have a secret identity in which he operated a sizeable business and technology infrastructure. It's difficult to keep these separate worlds completely apart, and not accidentally create some linkage between them. It's hard to stay anonymous for a long time while being active and engaging in a course of coordinated conduct working with other people over time. If there's ever a connection between those two identities say, if you slip up and use the name of one while wearing the mask of another, that link can never be destroyed and over time the different anonymous identities or mask that someone is trying to use tend to get connected.

Another lesson is that law enforcement can follow the money. Even before Ulbricht's arrest, the government knew that certain Bitcoin addresses were controlled by the operator of Silk Road, and they were watching those addresses. The result is that

Ulbricht, while wealthy according to the block chain, was not actually able to benefit from that wealth because any attempt to transfer those assets over into the dollar world would have resulted in a traceable event, and probably would have resulted in rapid arrest. So although Ulbricht was the owner of something like 174,000 bitcoins, the fact is is that he was not living like a king. He lived in a one-bedroom apartment in San Francisco while apparently unable to get to the wealth that he controlled.

In short, if you intend to operate an underground criminal enterprise and hope you don't then it's a lot harder to do then you might think. Technologies like Bitcoin and Tor are not panaceas for people who want to do these things and law enforcement has significant tools and resources that they can still use. Although there's been some panic in the world of law enforcement over the rise of Bitcoin, they are starting to realize that they can still follow the money up to a point and they still do have a substantial ability to investigate crimes and to make life difficult for people who want to engage in coordinated criminal action.

At the same time, to suggest that by taking down Silk Road, law enforcement has shut down Bitcoin-based hidden markets for illegal drugs for good. In fact, after the demise of Silk Road there has been a mushrooming of such markets. Some of the more prominent ones are Sheep Marketplace, Silk Road 2, Black Market Reloaded, Evolution, and Agora. Most of these are now defunct, either due to law-enforcement actions or due to theft, often by insiders. To address the security risk of the site operator disappearing with buyers' escrowed funds, the newer marketplaces use multi-signature escrow rather than Silk Road's model of depositing the funds with the market operator.

Anti-Money Laundering

Anti Money Laundering (AML) rules that governments have imposed, especially in the US, that effect some Bitcoin-related businesses.

The goal of anti-money-laundering policy is to prevent large flows of money from crossing borders or moving between the underground and legitimate economy without being detected. In some cases, countries are just fine with money crossing borders, but they want to know who's transferring what to whom and where that money came from.

Anti-money laundering is aimed at trying to make certain kinds of crime more difficult, especially organized crime. Organized crime groups often find themselves getting a lot of money coming in in one place and wanting to ship it somewhere else, but not wanting to explain where that money came from, hence the desire to get money across borders. Or they might find themselves making a lot of money in an underground economy and wanting to get that money into the legitimate economy so that they can spend it on sports cars and big houses or whatever it is that the leaders of the group want to do. Anti-money laundering, then, has the goals of making it harder to move money around this way and making it easier to catch people trying to do it.

Know Your Customer. One of the rules that goes with anti-money laundering is something called Know Your Customer, sometimes called KYC. The details can be a bit complicated and will depend on your locale, but the basic idea is this: Know Your Customer rules require certain kinds of businesses that handle money to do three things:

1. Identify and authenticate clients get some kind of authentication that clients really are

who they claim they are and that those claimed identities correspond to some kind of real-world identity. So a person can't just walk in and they're john Smith from 123 Main Street in AnyTown, USA. They have to provide an identity and have that be checked in order to engage in certain kinds of business.

2. Evaluate risk of client determine the risk of a certain client engaging in underground activities. This will be based on how the client behaves how longstanding their business relationship is with the company, how well known they are in the community, and various other factors. KYC rules generally require covered companies to treat clients whose activities seem riskier with more attention.

3. Watch for anomalous behavior that is, behavior that seems to be indicative of money laundering or criminal activity. KYC will often require a company to cut off business with a client who looks dodgy, or who is unable to authenticate themselves or their activities sufficiently for the rule.

Mandatory reporting.

There are mandatory reporting requirements in the United States that are worth talking about. Companies in a broad range of sectors have to report currency transactions that are over $10,000. They must file what's called a currency transaction report to say what the transaction is and who the other party to the transaction is. There is also some requirement to authenticate who that party is. Once reported, the information goes into government databases and then might be analyzed to look for patterns of behavior that are indicative of money laundering.

Companies are also required to watch for clients who might be "structuring" transactions to avoid reporting, like engaging in a series of $9,000 transactions to get around the $10,000 reporting rule. Companies that see evidence of structuring must report it by filing a Suspicious Activity Report. Again, the information goes into a government database and might lead to investigation of the client.

The requirements here differ by country. We're not by any means trying to give you legal advice about whether you need this or what you have to do. This discussion is meant to give you an idea about what kind of requirements are imposed by anti-money laundering rules. That said, take note that governments in the U.S. and other countries take anti-money laundering rules very, very seriously. These aren't the kind of rules that you can just blow off and deal with if you get a complaint from the government later.

Bitcoin businesses have been shut down sometimes temporarily, sometimes permanently. Business people have been arrested, and people have gone to jail for not following these rules. This is an area where government will enforce the law vigorously, regardless of whether fiat currency or Bitcoin is used. Government has enforced these laws against Bitcoin-based businesses ever since they noticed that Bitcoin was large enough to pose a risk of money laundering. If you're interested in starting any kind of business that will handle large volumes of currency, you'll need to talk to a lawyer who understands these rules.

Regulation

Now let's directly address the 'R' word — regulation. Regulation often gets a bad name, especially among the kind of people who tend to like Bitcoin. As the argument goes, regulation is some bureaucrat who doesn't know my business or what I'm trying to do, coming in and messing things up. It's a burden. It's stupid and pointless. This argument is pretty common and well understood, and it's often correct.

The bottom line argument in favor or regulation is this: when markets fail and produce outcomes that are bad and agreed to be bad by pretty much everyone in the market then regulation can step in and try to address the failure. So the argument for regulation, when there is an argument, starts with the idea that markets don't always give you the result that you'd like.

Lemons market.

One way in which the market can fail, a classic example called the lemons market. The name originated in the context of used cars. But let's talk about a market in concept, a market for "widgets," some kind of good that one wants to buy and sell. Let's say that widgets can either be of low quality or high quality. A high-quality widget costs a little bit more to manufacture than a low-quality widget, but it's much, much better for the consumer who buys it. Consumers like high-quality widgets a lot better.

If the market is operating well, if its efficient as economists call it, it will deliver mostly high-quality widgets to consumers. That's because even though the high-quality widget is a bit costlier, most consumers prefer it and are willing to pay more for it. So under certain assumptions a market will provide this happy outcome.

On the other hand, let's suppose customers can't tell apart a low-quality widget from a high-quality widget before buying it. The classic example is the used car. You're looking at a used car sitting on the lot, and it may look pretty good, but you can't really tell if it's going to break down tomorrow or if it's going to run for a long time. The dealer probably knows if it's a lemon, but you as the customer can't tell the difference.

The incentives that drive people in this kind of lemons market. As a consumer, you're not willing to pay extra for a high-quality widget, because you just can't tell the difference. Even if the used car dealer says that a car is perfect and is only an extra hundred dollars, you don't have a good reason to trust the dealer.

As a consequence, producers can't make any extra money by selling a high-quality widget. In fact, they lose money by selling a high-quality widget because it costs a bit more to produce and they don't get any price premium. So the market gets stuck at an equilibrium where only low-quality widgets are produced, and consumers are relatively unhappy with them.

This outcome is worse for everybody than a properly functioning market would be. It's worse for buyers because they have to make do with low-quality widgets. In a more efficient market they could have bought a widget that was much, much better for a slightly higher price. It's also worse for producers — since the widgets that are on the market are all lousy, consumers don't buy very many widgets. The widget market is relatively small, and so there's less money to be made selling widgets than there would be in a healthy market.

That's a market failure. This one, in particular, is a result of "asymmetric information" between buyers and sellers about the condition of the product. The resulting market is sometimes called a lemons market.

Fixing a lemons market.

There are some market-based approaches that try to fix a lemons market. The first relies on seller reputation. The idea is that if a seller consistently tells the truth to consumers about which widgets are high vs. low quality, then the seller might acquire a reputation for telling the truth. Once they have that reputation, they may be able to sell high-quality widgets for a higher price because consumers will believe them, and therefore the market can operate more efficiently.

This sometimes works and sometimes doesn't depending on the precise assumptions you make about the market. Of course, it will never work as well as a market where consumers can actually tell the difference in quality. For one thing, it takes a while for a producer to build up a good reputation. That means they have to sell high-quality widgets at low prices for a while until consumers learn that they're telling the truth. That makes it harder for an honest seller to get into the market.

The other potential problem is that a seller, even if they've been honest up to now, no longer has the incentive to be honest if they want to get out of the market (say, if their sales are shrinking). In that case their incentive is to massively cheat people all at once and then exit the market. So reputation doesn't work well at the beginning of a seller's presence is in the market as well as at the end.

A reputation-based approach also tends not to work in businesses where consumers don't do repeat business with the same entity, or where the product category is very new, and therefore there hasn't been enough time for sellers to build up a reputation. A high-tech market like Bitcoin exchanges suffers just those problems.

The other market-based approach is warranties. The idea is that a seller could provide a warranty to a buyer that says if the widget turns out to be low quality, the seller will provide an exchange or a refund. That can work well up to a point, but there's also a problem: a warranty is just another kind of product that can also come in high-quality or low-quality versions! A low-quality warranty is one where the seller doesn't really come through when you come back with the broken product. They renege on their promise or they make you jump through all kinds of hoops.

Regulatory fixes.

So if a lemons market has developed, and if these market-based approaches don't work for the particular market, then regulation might be able to help. Specifically, there are three ways in which regulation might be able to address the problem.

First, regulation could require disclosure. It could require, say, that all widgets be labeled as high quality or low quality, combined with penalties on the firms for lying. That gives consumers the information that they were missing. A second approach to regulation is to have quality standards so that no widget can be sold unless it meets some standard of quality testing, and to have that standard set so that only high-quality widgets can pass the test. That would result in a market that again has only one kind of widget, but at least it's high-quality widgets, assuming that the regulation works as intended. The third approach is to require all sellers to issue warranties and then enforce the operation of those warranties so that sellers are held to the promises that they make.

Any of these forms of regulation could obviously fail — it might not work as intended, might be mis-written or misapplied, or might be burdensome on sellers. But there's at least the possibility that regulation of this type might help to address the market failure due to a lemons market. People who argue for regulation of Bitcoin exchanges, for example, sometimes point to them as an example of a lemons market.

Collusion and antitrust law

Another example of markets not operating the way we would like them to is price fixing. Price fixing is when different sellers collude with each other and agree to raise prices or to not lower them. A related situation is where companies that would otherwise go into competition with each other agree not to compete. For example, if there were two bakeries in town they might agree that one of them will only sell muffins and the other will only sell bagels, and that way there's less competition between them then there would be if they both sold muffins and bagels. As a result of the reduced competition presumably prices go up, and the merchants are able to foil the operation of the market.

After all, the reason that the market protects consumers well in its normal operation is through the vehicle of competition. Sellers have to compete in order to offer the best goods at the best price to consumers, and if they don't compete in that way then they won't get business. An agreement to fix prices or to not compete circumvents that competition. When people take steps that prevent competition, that's another kind of market failure.

These kinds of agreements to raise prices or to not compete are illegal in most jurisdictions. This is part of antitrust law or competition law. The goal of this body of law is to prevent deliberate actions that prevent or harm competition. More generally, it limits actions other than simply offering good products at good prices, such as attempts to reduce competition through mergers. Antitrust law is very complicated and we've given you only a sketch of it, but it's another instance of how the market can fail and how the law can and will step in to prevent it.

CONCLUSION

With the advent of blockchain and cryptocurrencies being as new and revolutionary as it is, predicting the five-year projected value of either Bitcoin or Ethereum requires numerous factors to be considered. Through a combination of qualitative research conducted through interviews with industry professionals, linear regression, and a Monte Carlo analysis, it can be concluded that Bitcoin can leverage its existing user base and proven use case is likely to experience more growth in the five-year time horizon. Ethereum, while having a lower expected value has a much greater variance as a result of its strong correlation with speculation, news, and hype. Ethereum's wide range of outcomes, both positive and negative, indicate that it should be included in the investment portfolio to take advantage of this fact.

Bitcoin is a new Internet currency that anyone can get started mining. There are a number of reasons you might mine: for profit, to help secure the network, to help found a new Internet currency, or just to gain technical experience!

Throughout history, gold has had intrinsic value. The same can't always be said for paper based assets whose value is constantly fluctuating.

PROTECT YOUR WEALTH WITH GOLD.

ABOUT THE AUTHOR

Sir **Patrick** writes for the liberation of all people, focusing on the beautiful people who are often left out of cryptocurrency and the Bitcoin world, unaware they can invest and become a millionare. He is an Investment banker, Fund Manager. In addition to that, he is a senior banking redemption officer for the International Court of Justice and Judge.

Thank you again for purchasing this book, I hope you have enjoyed it!

Author: **SIR PATRICK BIJOU.**

REFERENCES

- Andy Greenberg (20 April 2011). "Crypto Currency". Forbes.com. Archived from the original on 31 August 2014. Retrieved 8 August 2014.
- Cryptocurrencies: A Brief Thematic Review Archived 2017-12-25 at the Wayback Machine... Economics of Networks Journal. Social Science Research Network (SSRN). Date accessed 28 august 2017.
- McDonnell, Patrick "PK" (9 September 2015). "What Is The Difference Between Bitcoin, Forex, and Gold". NewsBTC. Archived from the original on 16 September 2015. Retrieved 15 September 2015.
- Schueffel, Patrick (2017). The Concise Fintech Compendium. Fribourg: School of Management Fribourg/Switzerland. Archived from the original on 2017-10-24. "Cryptocurrency FAQ - What is

Distributed Ledger Technology?" Cryptocurrency Works. Retrieved 21 May 2018.

- Matteo D'Agnolo. "All you need to know about Bitcoin". Timesofindia economic times. Archived from the original on 2015-10-26.
- https://blockchaintraining.org/wpcon tent/uploads/2016/06/Wa rackMari-BlockchainsAndMoneyLaundering.pdf
- http://www.imperial.ac.uk/media/im perial-college/faculty-of engineering/computing/public/AlanVe y.pdf
- https://blockchaintraining.org/wpcon tent/uploads/2016/06/Scott-BlockchainStartupCompliance.compre ssed.pdf
- https://blockchaintraining.org/wpcon tent/uploads/2016/06/Salis-WorkingWithBitcoinInRuby.pdf
- https://blockchaintraining.org/wpcon tent/uploads/2016/06/Todd-CLTVCSV.compressed.pdf
- https://blockchaintraining.org/wpcon tent/uploads/2016/06/Lombrozo-SegregatedWitness.pdf
- https://blockchaintraining.org/wpcon tent/uploads/2016/06/Kiss-PycoinMultisig.pdf

- https://blockchaintraining.org/wpcon tent/uploads/2016/06/PerklinAntono poulos-CCSSInDepth.compressed.pdf
- https://www.youtube.com/watch?v=6 uXAbJQoZlE
- https://blockchaintraining.org/wpcon tent/uploads/2016/06/Cheng-CBP1.pdf
- https://blockchaintraining.org/wpcon tent/uploads/2016/06/Chamely-OmniPropertyIssuance.pdf
- https://blockchaintraining.org/wpcon tent/uploads/2016/06/Hoegner-LegalIssuesSurroundingBlockchainTok ens.pdf